NEW TOOLS
FOR
BUSINESS

A Quick Start Guide to
PODCASTING

D0024014

NEW TOOLS
FOR
BUSINESS

A Quick Start Guide to
PODCASTING

Creating your own audio
and visual material for iPods,
BlackBerries, mobile phones
and websites

Mark Harnett

KoganPage

LONDON PHILADELPHIA NEW DELHI

First published in Great Britain and the United States in 2010 by Kogan Page Limited

120 Pentonville Road	525 South 4th Street, #241	4737/23 Ansari Road
London N1 9JN	Philadelphia PA 19147	Daryaganj
United Kingdom	USA	New Delhi 110002
www.koganpage.com		India

© Mark Harnett, 2010

The right of Mark Harnett to be identified as the author of this work has been asserted by him in accordance with the Copyright, Designs and Patents Act 1988.

ISBN   978 0 7494 6145 4
E-ISBN 978 0 7494 6154 6

British Library Cataloguing-in-Publication Data

A CIP record for this book is available from the British Library.

Library of Congress Cataloging-in-Publication Data

Harnett, Mark.
    A quick start guide to podcasting : Creating your own audio and visual material for iPods, BlackBerries, mobile phones, and websites / Mark Harnett.
        p. cm.
    ISBN 978-0-7494-6145-4 — ISBN 978-0-7494-6154-6 (e-ISBN)   1. Webcasting.
2. Podcasting.   3. Mobile computing.   4. Internet marketing.   5. Multimedia communications.   I. Title.
    TK5105.887.H375 2010
    006.7'876—dc22

2010012750

Typeset by Graphicraft Limited, Hong Kong
Printed and bound in India by Replika Press Pvt Ltd

CONTENTS

INTRODUCTION: WHY PODCAST?

We live in exciting times. The internet is arguably the fastest growing cultural phenomenon in the world, *ever*. You and I are lucky enough to have been born in time to catch one of those moments in human history when everything changes. Right now we're in the middle of a communications revolution.

Being online is essential for your business. There simply isn't any other way to look at it. Even if you're the sort of person who still reads books (and you must be, because you're reading this one), buys a daily newspaper and watches the six o'clock news on television, you can't afford to be left behind as your competitors elbow past you online.

So you already have a website. Great. (If you haven't, you might want to get hold of our book on Google AdWords to help you set one up.) Why would you need anything more than that?

Because, in the world of online business nothing stands still. You have to be continually changing and modifying and improving to stay one jump ahead.

Revolutions are almost always driven by technology. When the tools reach the hands of the masses, that's when the world changes. Prehistorians will tell you it was the invention of the plough that turned us from nomadic hunter-gatherers to settled city dwellers. The internal combustion engine began the transport revolution of the 20th century, but it was Henry Ford's mass-production of his model-T car that really set us free to go where we wanted. Behind the current phase of the digital revolution is the rapid evolution of ever more mobile, portable computing technology. That's why you need to consider podcasting as a way of promoting your business.

It was Apple's invention of the iPod that made podcasting possible. Initially the iPod was simply another digital device that gave people a way to access their favourite music on the move and other manufacturers were quick to follow with their own MP3 audio players. As the first in the field, the iPod lent its name to the process of making available for mass consumption download any kind of audio, music or speech. Broadcasters were quick to spot the potential of 'listen again' for radio programmes but podcasting took the process a step further. Listeners could download audio material to their MP3 players to listen on the move; they didn't have to be tied to their desktop computer or even to a laptop.

Although initially confined to audio this restriction was quickly removed. The devices got smaller while their memory capacity increased allowing video files to be downloaded too. Although for a while it became fashionable to use the term 'vodcasting' to describe the visual equivalent now most people use podcasting to encompass both audio and video downloads, and that is what we'll do in this book.

To start with it was younger people who took the greatest advantage of podcasting technology but gradually the older generation have joined in. There must have been a similar turning point when the portable transistor radio was invented back in the 1960s. At first it might have seemed that the only sound that could be heard on a portable audio device was pop music. But now even your granddad has probably realized he can download his favourite radio programmes to listen to when he walks the dog, and grandma has worked out it's a lot easier plugging the MP3 player into the car lighter socket than carting an armful of CDs back and forth when she's driving to the shops.

Still, some might argue it's fiddly to download audio or video material from your computer and onto a portable device. The kids might do it but can the average busy person really find the time?

Well, that might have been true once but now technology is moving on again and driving another phase of the revolution. Instead of buying specialized, dedicated devices like the iPod, increasing numbers of people on the move use their mobile phones as a multi-purpose communications and entertainment device. The holy grail of digital technology, the all-purpose handheld gizmo, is almost with us. The latest phones offer not only cameras but high quality video capture, FM radio and enough memory to store your entire music collection, e-mails and text. As well as interfacing easily with your computer at home, you can access the internet on the move through the phone and download virtually what you want, where you want, when you want. And it won't stop here. The devices will become more efficient, more lightweight, cheaper, easier to use.

So look again at your business's web presence. If you want to reach a younger generation of customers or clients, those who are the 'early adopters' of the latest technology, you should be podcasting already. But even if your customer base is more mature, it won't be long before they too are accessing your website via their mobile phone.

'Stuff and nonsense,' says my sweet old-fashioned aunt, 'You might do these things, nephew dear, but you can't tell me that I'll be accessing the internet via my mobile phone any day soon. What would I want to do that for?'

Oh yes you will, auntie. You soon got the hang of texting, didn't you? Not only are humans adaptable creatures but the drive is always for the mass of the technology to get simpler and easier to use. You'll be wandering round your favourite park accessing a website to find out the name of that lovely crimson rose cascading over the pergola, and where you can buy one for your own garden. And because when you sit down on the park bench to read the details on the small screen, you realize you've forgotten your glasses, dear auntie, you might even find it easier to access some of the information in audio mode.

We have been brought up to think that reading the written word is the best means of assimilating information, and indeed reading has many advantages. Reading a message is quicker than listening to the same message and it is easy to glance back and read something over again to clarify and understand it.

But effective communication is about horses for courses. There will be times, especially when people are on the move, when an audio or video message exactly hits the spot. There are some things, for instance, that simply beg to be seen. While I was writing the book on Google AdWords, I talked to a farmer's wife who had successfully used AdWords to attract visitors to her website promoting her business selling organically reared geese. But she'd also realized that using words to describe the conditions in which the geese were raised was not enough. Her customers wanted to see for themselves. So she filmed her geese wandering free-range in the apple orchard where they spend most of their days, and uploaded a clip to her website. Sales soared.

Convinced yet? You should be. Whether you're a farmer's wife or a fundraiser, an artist or an artisan, a musician or a manufacturer, a shop or a service, a global corporation or a neighbourhood charity, podcasting can enhance your website. No matter what kind of business you're in you will find it useful. It gives your brand more than an Internet presence; it gives it a *voice*. It will help you establish a corporate, commercial or individual identity. You'll find that you can use a podcast to reach a different demographic than you've previously been able to tap into. If you get it right and make the podcast so interesting and compelling that people want to share it with each other, you'll find it's a way of enticing potential customers or clients to your website.

Although you might think that video trumps audio every time, you'd be wrong. If that were so, radio would have died a few years after television was invented. Indeed, plenty of people back then thought it would. But radio still thrives. Audio podcasting can be just as effective as video and still has its place. After all, when people are on the move, they may not be able to devote all their senses to communication. You might be able to watch video on the train or plane, but you can't walk along the street with your eyes glued to a small screen without running the risk of bumping into something, and you certainly can't drive your car at the same time as watching video. But you can listen, and that's why audio podcasting is often especially effective as a means of reaching people who'll download material they don't have time to read and take it with them on their daily commute or when they go for a run or to the gym.

We'll look at both audio and video podcasting in this book, through examples of people who have found how useful podcasting can be to help their business grow. Podcasting is a phenomenon so new and exciting that there are no hard and fast rules, although there are certainly guidelines that can help you make a success of it. What I want to do is to give you enough help to start you off:

then it's up to you to be creative. It doesn't matter whether you want to reach a global market, or simply speak to a few dozen people. Podcasting can help you establish your own online identity and community.

It's not difficult either. Mass communication was once regarded as an esoteric craft, a matter for professionals. There was a kind of Brahmin class of 'experts' who were the only ones who knew how to use the specialized equipment that made broadcasting possible. But you don't have to invest thousands, or even hundreds, to make a podcast possible. You can even upload video captured on your mobile phone, though it's true if you spend a little money the results may be easier on the eye and the ear. Often the most successful podcasts have been those incorporating a clever and creative idea that has somehow captured the zeitgeist – the spirit of the times.

We'll start simple by devoting the first part of the book to audio. Second for second, audio files are smaller than video. I'll show you how easy it is to devise and create your own sound podcast, recording and editing it yourself before uploading it to your own website or to a site like iTunes where it can attract new visitors to your site. In the second half of the book we'll look at how to make a video podcast for use on your website and via networking sites such as YouTube.

All you need to start is a little imagination and even if you're stumped for ideas the examples I'll share with you should help to set your imagination free.

PART I
AUDIO

CHAPTER 1
HOW TO WRITE FOR THE EAR

CASE STUDY

Sarah Shrubb and *Corduroy Mansions*

Sarah Shrubb has a wonderful job. She reads novels in the office. Of course she has to work as well because she's an Editorial Director at publishers Little, Brown, where one of the most esteemed fiction authors is the Scottish writer Alexander McCall Smith. He's written over 60 books including the global best-selling *No.1 Ladies' Detective Agency* series. For some time he's been serializing his stories in *The Scotsman*, so last year he decided to do the same thing with a UK national newspaper, *The Daily Telegraph*. They were very keen to publish his serialization, *Corduroy Mansions*, on their website.

It's not possible to become an international best-selling author unless you can tell great stories. To create a story that works in a serialisation format another talent is needed, an ability to create what Sarah describes as 'lovely vignettes with cliff hangers', but what is more, Alexander McCall Smith has another talent that makes him a natural for podcasting. He writes to be read aloud. He has perfect pacing and characters that are real to life, both heroes and villains, and all his stories have humour that makes you laugh out loud. In *Corduroy Mansions* he created a parallel world in which a cast of mostly likeable, fallible characters tried to do the right thing by their neighbours living in a four-storey building in Pimlico, London.

The UK and the USA have a tradition of serializing audio books. In the UK it extends from Radio 4's Book of the Week to Woman's Hour. But *Corduroy Mansions* was the first time that text and audio were simultaneously serialized in a newspaper. With one hundred podcasts the reader/listener had the option either to read the text or listen. It was online in the written form on *The Daily Telegraph*'s website but also available via iTunes in audio form. Quite often audio editions are cut to a specific, shortened length, but because the material was podcast alongside the serialization in the newspaper, it was completely unabridged.

Sarah has considerable experience in the world of audio podcasting and thinks that for fiction the ideal length of script is between 1,000 and 1,300 words or about 15 and 20 minutes of recorded time. She explained:

> *In fiction the reader needs time to get into the character build-up and character description. You need enough of the story for it to be gripping and then build up your climax and then have a cliff hanger. So you need at least a story in each piece. For other podcasts I think perhaps they could be a little shorter.*

She became an expert in the logistics of manuscript delivery and recording:

> *Sandy was literally writing as he went. He hadn't got the book prepared. We'd get say 10 chapters here, 20 chapters there and then we would edit and record them. Then release them according to plan. Everything was done*

*with very tight planning. The terrible thing with this would
have been to reach a point where your podcasts have
run out and we'd have to say to the listeners 'sorry'.
Or worst case scenario – the text was available but
the recording wasn't. That would have been awful.*

The strength of the podcasts was revealed in the community building around it as each podcast was launched online. People could write in and comment about the characters and say 'this is happening, that is happening'. And the author could respond.

Sarah believes that if a first time fiction author wanted to showcase work with a podcast it would be 'absolutely fine' to record the story read by themself. But a major publisher has exacting standards and the podcasts used the established actor Andrew Sachs to read the stories. She considers:

*It's incredibly hard to do and you need someone who has
training and skill who can come up with voices for
characters and then just slip into character. It's amazing
to watch in the studio, the actor is having a conversation
with himself in different voices. It's very, very, skilled.
I think an author can often read non-fiction very well
but fiction can be quite hard unless they're already
a trained vocal actor.*

The podcast series was a success and *Corduroy Mansions II* is to follow. What's more, the podcast did not cannibalize sales, in fact it worked as a marketing tool for the audio book which has sold commercially. This isn't unusual as podcasts are viewed by marketers as 'value added content'; they create exposure that develops online awareness and builds customer loyalty.

The simplest form of podcast is a single voice conveying a story to the listener's ear. Sarah Shrubb's example can help you with understanding how to make your audio podcast listenable and compelling.

People respond to **stories**. A story, in words or pictures, conveys a message more effectively than anything else; you only have to think how the world's major faiths often use stories in the form of parables or myths to convey philosophical truths and religious tenets. Jesus was a storyteller and so too are most gurus and prophets.

CREATE YOUR STORY

So when you're deciding what your podcast should be, think in terms of constructing a story. It could be the story of your brand: how your company started, how that reflects your special philosophy. It might be the day-to-day story of what is happening in your organization, a kind of spoken blog. It might be the story of your product, or the story of how you were able to help one of your clients.

Sarah describes Alexander McCall Smith as a 'born storyteller', but we all have storytelling hard-wired into our brains. It's not difficult. You probably tell stories all the time, unselfconsciously, to your friends and family. 'You'll never guess what happened at work today...'

And people love listening to stories. But we do distinguish between the kind of stories that hold our attention and those that don't. A good story needs to be:

- vivid;
- exciting;
- engaging;
- to the point – it shouldn't ramble.

For instance, I'm often asked how long a podcast should be. The answer is any length, provided it's the right length for the particular kind of material. People say that attention spans are getting shorter but that's probably not true. What is happening is that the things people are prepared to give their attention to have changed. If they're excited and intrigued by a clever and interesting story, they'll spend longer with it. If they're bored, or simply not interested in the kind of message you're communicating, they won't be polite and wait to hear you out. They'll melt away into cyber-space long before you've finished.

What's as important as length is the shape of the story. This is what makes it interesting and exciting. It may sound obvious to say that a good story has a beginning, a middle and an end, but that's exactly what boring storytellers forget.

HOOK YOUR LISTENER

The **beginning** is the hook that grabs the listeners and makes them want to listen on. You have to catch them with the first few sentences. For example, compare:

'I have always been interested in pecuniary matters and accountancy...'

with

'It was the day my father cut off my pocket money that I decided I'd train as a financial consultant...'

The first is a description, and not a very interesting one. The second is the start of a story. Why did dad cut off the cash? What terrible crime had our narrator committed?

The **middle** is the main body of the story. Here your job is to keep the listener interested. So the story should have twists and turns, surprises and suspense, though it mustn't ramble.

And finally, the story has to have a point to which it is moving, in other words, the **end**. So, without wishing to plunge into the full technicalities of narrative theory, even the simplest form of podcast is going to take some planning. Well before you start recording, you need to ask yourself what you're trying to achieve and how you intend to use the podcast to get your message across. What is the story you want to tell about your business?

Make some notes about your 'story' and the shape it will have before you begin writing because you almost certainly will be writing this kind of podcast, rather than speaking off the cuff or 'ad-libbing'. As many broadcasters will tell you, unless you are a very unusual and gifted individual indeed, the best ad-libs are the ones you prepare in advance.

FIND THE RIGHT WORDS

'I can tell you what turns me off some podcasts,' says writer and broadcaster Jenni Mills. 'Long, complicated sentences, pompous, overblown language: in other words the kind of grammar and syntax that makes it impossible to follow what the podcaster is trying to get across.'

What many people fail to realize is that there's a difference between writing for the page, and writing for the ear. Jenni knows about both because she's a novelist who teaches creative writing to MA students, but has also worked for many years in radio and television.

'Simplicity is the key,' she says. 'If the words are on a page or a screen, the reader's eye can go back over some particularly complicated thought or sentence and puzzle it out. But the ear has only one chance to grasp the meaning.

If you don't make your point clearly in a podcast, the listener won't rewind. They'll switch off.'

When you've settled on what you want to say, write it in the simplest, clearest language you can. Podcasting isn't an exercise in showing off how impressive your vocabulary is, or the peerless beauty of your poetic skills. The language and grammar you use must be simple enough for listeners to grasp at first hearing. Using big words and complex grammar has a distancing effect for the people you're hoping to reach through your podcast. It makes you sound over-keen to impress, or stiff and formal.

English is a fabulously rich language. It evolved from many roots – Norman French, Germanic Anglo-Saxon, Viking Norse and Latin, which was the language used by churchmen, the learned, and was the language of law and government in ancient times. So we often have several different words that will do pretty much the same job, though sometimes with subtle shifts in meaning – 'emancipated', 'liberated', and 'free', for instance. Basically, the principle is you shouldn't use a long word when there's a shorter one that means the same thing, and you shouldn't use an elaborate one when there's a better word in more common use.

Take the words 'emaciated' and 'thin'. There's a subtle difference between them, but many people misuse 'emaciated' when the word 'thin' would do perfectly well. Unless you really mean painfully, abnormally, slender, you would be better to use 'thin' in a podcast. Thin is a more everyday word. It has one syllable, but emaciated has five. And are you sure you know how it is pronounced – 'ee-may-ciated', or 'emm-ass-iated'? The dictionary will tell you.

To take an even simpler example: 'however', and 'but'. Both mean exactly the same thing. As a general rule, it's better to use 'but' because it's shorter and less formal, so sounds more conversational. This isn't 'talking down' to your listeners. Clearly you wouldn't want them to imagine you're using words of one syllable because you believe they're not capable of understanding anything more complex. Longer words aren't absolutely forbidden, but you need to be using them as you would in everyday conversation.

WRITING STYLE

You don't have to worry about perfect grammar. No one is really going to care if you split an infinitive.

But you should avoid over-complicated sentence construction, involving lots of subordinate clauses. If you try to cram so many facts and ideas and thoughts into the sentence that you end up with an impossibly long and tottering structure, full of little asides hanging off each other like distant cousins on a particularly elaborate family tree, with a new thought here, which is meant to reinforce your main point, followed by a particularly striking metaphor that just occurred to you, another aside there (not to mention the odd phrase in brackets) that makes the whole thing so difficult to follow that... Um. I'm lost.

Keep it short. If it's a new thought, start a new sentence. Avoid too many 'whichs' and 'thats'. Put in a full stop instead. You're aiming for a friendly, conversational, informal style.

Here's an example of how not to do it:

Articulating the diverse needs of the indigenous peoples of sub-Saharan Africa is the task which the organization has set itself. Since the inception of the current strategies in 2003, the administrative body has been mindful of the underlying political tensions and geo-physical challenges in the region, which have underpinned all the policy decisions taken by the present board, while allowing some necessary flexibility in the arrangements for the delivery and distribution of non-governmental aid, and it has been increasingly incumbent upon charities like ourselves to process the most imperative requests for assistance with reference to, effectively, a triage process.

How about this instead? A story, told in simple words:

Kia is 12. She's never known life free from war or famine. In her village in the Sudan, the most pressing concern is when the next lorry-load of food will arrive. Will she and her mother manage to fight their way to the front of the crowd to grab a few precious handfuls of rice and keep her baby brother alive? Helping Kia and her family is our charity's main job. We have to be ready to move the aid at a moment's notice to wherever it is most needed.

So here in summary are the dos and don'ts of writing for podcast.

DO use:

- everyday, unpretentious vocabulary;
- short sentences;
- simple grammar;
- direct, active language;
- personalized stories.

DON'T use:

- unnecessarily big words. Words with one or two syllables are better than those with three or four!
- long involved sentences containing several different ideas;

- complex grammar with lots of interwoven sub-clauses – these are very difficult for the listener to follow;
- passive, impersonal language;
- abstract thinking without examples.

'People will understand you better and like you more if you use simple grammar and language,' says Jenni. 'Not only that, but you'll be glad you did when you come to record the piece. It's so much easier to voice a script if it's simply written. Fewer syllables and shorter sentences equal more breath and a stronger, more confident sound!'

Talking of which...

FIND THE RIGHT VOICE

Sarah Shrubb used an actor to bring the *Corduroy Mansions* podcast to life. Apart from the fact that Alexander McCall Smith is a busy man, in a professional production of an audio book an actor does a different and arguably better job than the author.

But there's no reason why you shouldn't be the voice of your own podcast. In fact you are probably the best person to do it. Not only do you know what you want to convey, it will come from your heart.

You don't have to have a beautiful voice, or put on a posh accent. All you require is confidence in what you're saying. The most important advice is to be yourself, and talk to your invisible listeners as if they were just across the table from you.

'It doesn't take a special talent,' says Jenni Mills, who has trained some of the best known broadcasters in the UK. 'The only trick is to think of yourself as explaining your thoughts to one person, rather than reading in front of an audience. When people read, they often sound flat and dull. But if you can think of yourself as *talking* the piece, it will sound much more exciting and lively.'

You might find it helpful to have a friend or colleague sit opposite you while you record the podcast, so that you can talk to them and 'lift the words off the page' as the broadcasters say. Pick someone who won't make you giggle though. The key to success is to relax and enjoy yourself while making the recording. Above all, don't worry about it. The more confident you feel, the more confident you'll sound.

But what if you hate the sound of your own voice, and would rather have your teeth extracted with rusty pliers than sit in front of a microphone speaking to the world? If you really don't want to tackle the job yourself, and you have the budget, you could find a professional voice to record your podcast. Although actors can do a brilliant job and as Sarah Shrubb says, make the best audio-book readers, for a straightforward factual podcast which doesn't need the performance element you might find a broadcaster will do as good a job, if not better. They are practised in being themselves in front of a microphone and sounding natural.

The cost of using a professional voice will vary, depending on how long the job takes and how well known the name of the broadcaster or actor. Experienced voice artists are expensive, because you're paying for the fact that listeners will recognize and feel familiar with their voice. But there may be an eager young broadcaster at your local radio station who could do the job for you much more cheaply. But whether you employ a professional voice or tackle the job yourself, remember it all comes back to the story you want to tell about your business.

Find the right story, and the world will listen.

TOP TIPS FOR WRITING FOR AUDIO

▶ Think in terms of constructing a story

▶ Check your podcast has a beginning, middle and end

▶ Make your point clearly

▶ Write in simple clear language

▶ Think of yourself as explaining your thoughts to one person, rather than reading in front of an audience

QUESTION

▶ What value will you add to your material by creating an audio pod cast?

ACTION

▶ Audio podcasts are only worth creating if you have an interesting story to tell. You will not be able to create exposure for your ideas or build customer loyalty if the basic material is dull. That doesn't mean that everyone will find it interesting – you may have a specialist interest group that is excited by what you have to say, but whatever your subject matter, you need to tell a great story.

CHAPTER 2
HOW TO INTERVIEW

CASE STUDY

The Beautiful Game **Podcast**

In early 2006, Alex Rice and three friends decided to start their own weekly football podcast. 'It was my friend Alex Kunawicz's idea initially,' explains Alex. 'This was still pretty early days for podcasting and he was frustrated by the lack of really good football podcasts, so he thought it might be fun to set one up together.'

One joint purchase later of a mid-priced Marantz digital recorder and the team were in business. They decided to name their show *The Beautiful Game* after the famous quote by legendary Brazilian footballer Pelé, and their aim was to offer an overview of all the results, stories and controversy of every English Premier League weekend.

Although all four members of the team work as researchers and journalists for the BBC, their expertise didn't necessarily include technical know-how. 'We used an Apple Mac for our editing and to be honest it was trial and error, especially at first,' admits Alex. 'We soon found our way, though, and we became more ambitious by encouraging interaction with our listeners.

They sent in jingles and left phone messages and we also displayed on our website photos taken at games.'

A format began to grow as they developed ideas for segments within the programme:

> *One of our main sections was called 'One Minute Match' where we would take each of the weekend's games in turn and very quickly explain the key incidents inside a minute, which was a really effective way of getting all our listeners up to speed without boring those who might already have seen the goals or read the reports. We also had the 'Half-Time Cuppa,' which was the four of us taking a single theme, like football films or the best World Cup games of all time, and simply discussing and arguing about them for a few minutes.*

The Beautiful Game also regularly presented interviews, featuring names few of their competitors could hope to attract:

> *Admittedly, we shamelessly used our contacts to snare a few good names! I remember our first interview was with journalist Mick Dennis of* The Daily Express, *but we also spoke with former Crystal Palace forward Mark Bright, former Spurs striker and regular BBC pundit Garth Crooks and former Liverpool and Republic of Ireland defender, Mark Lawrenson, who has been one of the BBC's main football analysts for many years. We always conducted the interviews person-to-person, usually in an office, with one or occasionally two people asking the questions. Often we would be interviewing them for a specific reason. For example, the Mark Lawrenson interview was specifically set as a preview piece ahead of a big European Champions League game for his old club Liverpool. It helped us to stay disciplined with our line of questioning. Having said that, these were generally*

relaxed football chats – we weren't setting out to really grill anyone.

Within weeks, it was clear that the show had found a gap in the market as downloads steadily increased. One particular high point was the 2006 World Cup. 'Three of us were in Germany with the BBC, which was hard enough work, but we decided to try and squeeze in a podcast every two or three days as well. Our other presenter was so dedicated, he even flew out specifically to help record the show.'

The Beautiful Game received downloads from all over the world, including Australia, Europe and all over Asia, but the real hits were coming from the States: 'I think it became popular with ex-pat Brits who didn't get to see *Match of the Day* any more. Our Facebook group also took off and a lot of our members were logging on from across the Atlantic.'

At their peak, they received an incredible 10,000 downloads in one week, were in the Top 20 of the iTunes chart and were even featured on iTunes' front page. Even now, *The Beautiful Game* archive is still available to download and has over 40 positive reviews, boasting a four-and-a-half star rating.

Dark clouds were forming, though. 'Time was becoming an issue,' says Alex. 'It would take us two solid days to produce and it was becoming too much for us to continue unless there was some way to make money out of it.'

The team did look into various ways of capitalizing on their success:

We asked Tetley's tea company if they wanted to sponsor the 'Half-Time Cuppa' segment, but we weren't successful there. We looked into teaming with BBC Worldwide but there were various issues that stopped that idea and we even considered selling Beautiful Game merchandise online, but the maths just didn't add up. We had a good

*meeting with one company who were willing to add us to
their books and start charging the price of a cup of coffee
per download, but even they admitted that would cost us
90 per cent of our audience. Eventually, we realized we had
to bring the series to an end. Most other football podcasts
were backed by newspapers and we simply didn't have
their resources.*

So in August 2007, *The Beautiful Game* was brought to
a reluctant end:

*We had a lot of e-mails asking us to continue, but it wasn't
possible. It was a great experience, one we all enjoyed,
but deciding to make a weekly podcast is an enormous
commitment. If you do manage to establish a base of
listeners, they really expect the show to be delivered on
time every week and eventually we just could not afford
to give up that kind of time.*

Writing a piece for a podcast isn't the only way of telling
the story of your product or business. You could record
a conversation, an interview perhaps, with one of your
clients or suppliers, or someone else who works for or
with your organization, so that it is they who tell the story
for you.

In some ways, using an interview as the basis of your
podcast looks much easier than writing something. But as
any television or radio journalist will tell you, it isn't always
as easy as you think. Before going any further, let's assess
the pros and cons of both methods of producing material
for your podcast.

Both methods take time and planning if you want a
good result. All the 'negatives', like written pieces sounding too formal, or interviews going out of control and

Written piece	Interview
Takes time to plan and write	Contrary to what most people think, good interviews also take time to plan and prepare!
Can sound stiff and formal unless you work hard at making the writing and the delivery as natural as possible	Can sound more conversational and natural, if you pick the right person to talk to
You have much more control over the message	You are dependent upon the person interviewed saying what you hoped they would say... but you can edit the interview to cut out the parts that don't work!

not saying what you hoped they would can be easily overcome, if you're prepared. And, as with just about everything in life, the more often you do something the easier it becomes. If you make a few mistakes to start off with, don't be discouraged – that's how even the best interviewers learned their craft. If it doesn't sound right to you, you don't have to put the podcast up on the website until you're absolutely satisfied it's exactly what you want.

Although this chapter falls into the audio section of the book, the interviewing guidelines and techniques explained here apply equally to any interview filmed for a video podcast. Pretty much all of it is basic common sense, not rocket science, and although I've drawn on advice from the professionals in radio and TV, it's as easy as... having a chat with someone. Basically, an interview on audio or video is just a recorded conversation and what could feel easier and more natural than that?

WHO TO INTERVIEW

As Alex Rice and friends discovered after they had created *The Beautiful Game*, it's very hard to persuade people to pay for content online, though there are a few examples where that has worked. You're unlikely to make additional revenue out of the podcast itself; think of it as a way to attract people to your online market stall.

The reason for having an interview in a podcast is to tell a story that will be helpful and appealing to your customers or clients, and that will draw other people to your website. Choosing the right person is key. The footballers in the example above were celebrities whose voices people wanted to hear, so that attracted more visitors to the website.

Famous names, if you happen to be in the kind of business where you encounter them, can certainly be very effective. Fans Google the names of their idols and trawl the internet looking for their latest appearances online. But don't get carried away and start e-mailing every star name in your address book, even supposing you have any, which I certainly don't. Just because you once played a charity football match alongside a top DJ, or once sold a sports car to Rio Ferdinand's wife, you can't assume they will have any interest in lending their name to promote your business for free. Trust me, you couldn't afford to pay top celebrity rates.

Besides, you always need to keep at the back of your mind the reason for the podcast. Are the celebrity's fans the ideal demographic for your product or service? Increased traffic to your website because a famous client has generously offered a testimonial – 'I only trust Sarah at Happy Hair to do my highlights before the Brit Awards' – would be marvellous, but only if it generates genuine increased business you are ready to cope with. There's useful traffic and there's time-wasting traffic; the latter being the kind that doesn't win you more orders, and crashes your website because you weren't prepared for it.

So for those of us who don't take tea with Robbie Williams on a regular basis, or have Johnny Depp's unlisted number, who else might you choose to interview?

Clearly this depends on the kind of business you're in. A charity might choose from its clients if they were willing to tell their story. A physiotherapist or a chiropractor might be able to persuade a satisfied client to talk about how they had been helped. Clients are often very grateful for what you have done for them, and their personal stories can encourage other people with similar problems to seek out your help.

If you're thinking of interviewing a client, I hardly need remind you about issues of confidentiality. There may not be appear to be a problem in the examples I've just given, assuming the clients have freely consented to the interview and understand how it will be used on the website. But do make sure they realize that people all over the world will have access to their story. Respect whatever degree of anonymity they ask for. Remember too that using a client in this way may send out the wrong message to other clients if you work in a particularly sensitive field. Prospective clients might think that by using your services they too could be asked to go public with their problems. Even in less sensitive areas you need to judge carefully which clients would be open to an approach and who would be good at telling a story that will help promote your business. Many people are very willing to help if they can, but talking about yourself on record requires a degree of extroversion. You need to look for confident, articulate speakers who have the gift of the gab and can describe things in an interesting, colourful way.

This is true for anyone else you might pick to interview. As television and radio producers will tell you, the people who make the best programmes are those who might be described as 'characters', who can talk vividly about themselves and their activities, and won't clam up when the microphone appears. Suppose for instance you run an online business selling handmade knitwear. You might choose to pick one of the chatty home knitters who produces the garments for you. Or even the couple running a smallholding in the Welsh mountains, whose rare breed of sheep provide some of the wool. Both could provide an interesting story that enhances your business; customers love to know the story behind the products they buy. But before you drive hundreds of miles to record them, have a long conversation with them over the phone first and make sure they're as chatty and as interesting as you remember.

You might, alternatively, be looking for the kind of expert whose authoritative testimony will add value to your brand. If you manufacture a revolutionary new type of foam mattress designed for back sufferers, you might think it a good idea to put up on your site a downloadable podcast of back care advice and exercise regimes from top osteopath Dr Wilhelm von Spine. He may be the leading man in his field, but make sure first his German accent isn't so impenetrable that no one listening will understand him.

It's this kind of planning and preparation, well before you set up the microphone to start recording, that will pay dividends and save you time and wasted effort in the long run. If you've ever been involved in the making of a radio or television programme you may have noticed that often the researchers spend a lot of time talking to prospective interviewees beforehand to be sure they are exactly the right kind of people for the programme. If you don't fit the bill, you won't hear from them again.

So whoever you pick to interview, be sure to pick someone who:

- is happy to do it;
- sounds warm, friendly and chatty – ideally your customers will need to like them and identify with them;
- won't be too nervous and dry up in front of the microphone;
- has a good story or stories to tell;
- or – depending on what the podcast is for – is an authoritative expert in their field whose information can enhance your product or service.

THE INTERVIEWER'S ROLE

At the risk of your kicking this book across the room for stating the blessed obvious, interviews, you may have noticed, take TWO people. There's the person being interviewed and giving the answers, the interviewee, and the person asking the questions, the interviewer. You'd be surprised how often people forget this.

You'll be very lucky indeed if you simply sit your interviewee down, turn on the microphone, smile encouragingly, and they start speaking. You'd be even more lucky if they carried on doing so engagingly and interestingly without a stumble or fluff for some 8 or 10 minutes, saying everything you hoped they would say, and then drawing their monologue to a graceful conclusion with the perfect exit line.

This just doesn't happen in the real world. You have to work to get a good interview. So you need to arm yourself with a list of questions that will prompt the kind of answers you want the interviewee to give you.

And do remember we're talking about questions here – not statements of what *you* think. You are the interviewer, which means your job is to prompt and encourage the person you're interviewing, not to take over the interview and answer the questions yourself.

Knowing how much of yourself to allow into the interview is a difficult balance to strike. Some of the professionals who interview for a living on radio and television are entirely self-effacing and you'd hardly know they were there, except for the occasional penetrating question that steers the interview in the direction they've planned it to go. Just because you don't hear much from them doesn't mean they've abdicated control of the interview. Others are much more present, pushing and jostling verbally, making jokes and steering the conversation in an obvious fashion. When it's not done well you wish they'd shut up, and let the other guy talk. But sometimes this technique produces a hilariously entertaining dialogue where both interviewer and interviewee are bouncing off each other and so clearly having a good time that it's great to listen to.

Either way of interviewing is valid – provided it gets you the result you want, which is an entertaining or thought-provoking piece of audio that will promote your enterprise. But one style of interview that almost certainly has no place in a promotional podcast is the confrontation: the kind practised by tough news-and-current-affairs journalists who are taking politicians or bad guys to task. Here it's entirely inappropriate:

So, Karen, your job here is to pack the widgets into boxes before dispatch to our customers?

Er, yes, Mr Tyler...

And would you say that you always get them out on time to meet the order date?

Well, um, we try, but...

But you don't always succeed, then? What do you do if the order is dispatched late?

Well, er, I think, you send the customer an e-mail, don't you, and waive the postage and packing?

You think? You think*? Shouldn't you KNOW, Karen?*

THE INTERVIEW RELATIONSHIP

An interview is a relationship between two people. In some interview relationships the interviewee should be predominant, in others the interviewer will be more proactive. But the watchword in this kind of conversational relationship is generosity. The interviewer's role is to allow the interviewee to shine. If you're going to be the kind of interviewer who makes jokes and jollies the interviewee along, do make sure you are really as funny as you think. There's nothing more cringe-making than an interviewer who thinks they are talent-show material, and swamp the much more interesting tale the interviewee has to tell.

WHAT TO ASK

I once asked a professional interviewer how she worked out what questions to ask. Did she sit down and make a list of questions, and switch them around until she felt she had the order right?

'Oh, I never start with the questions,' she said. 'I start with the *answers*.'

This isn't as cock-eyed as it sounds. What she meant was that before she begins an interview she has to have a clear idea of what she wants from the finished piece of audio. This saves a huge amount of time, because the interview will then not ramble and take days to edit into a coherent shape.

As I suggested earlier, time spent talking to the interviewee beforehand is never wasted, it's essential. That way you find out in advance what they have to say, what are their best anecdotes, what are the memorable phrases they use which you want them to repeat again when the recording begins. Those were the things the professional interviewer noted down as part of her research process and then moved around like the pieces of a jigsaw puzzle to make a coherent 'story' for her interview. When she was satisfied that she knew the answers that she wanted to elicit from the interviewee and the order in which they would work best, only then did she settle to work out what questions would produce exactly those answers and draw up a list.

'And don't forget to ask *open* questions,' she added. 'That's really important. You need to ask questions your interviewee can't simply answer yes or no to.'

Open questions are those that begin with words like who, what, where, and how? These encourage the interviewees to expand on what they have to say. Closed questions, on the other hand, tend to reduce the possible answer to a simple positive or negative. Instead of:

'Are you busy in the warehouse at weekends?'

'Yes.'

Try instead:

'When are the busiest moments in the warehouse?'

'Well, weekends are the time we really earn our money. Everybody is online then, placing orders that need to be dispatched as soon as possible, and we pride ourselves that we get every single one on the road before Monday morning...'

Or you might think of replacing...

'Are you happy sheep-farming?'

'Yes.'

...with the more open:

'How much do you love your work?'

'Oh, this has to be the best job in the world! Look at that view from the pasture. There's a million shades of green on this mountainside. The sheep can be awkward buggers, but they've all got their own individual characters. That's Larry over there, we bottle-fed him, and he's never forgotten it, always trots over and butts you in the stomach...'

You can see how the closed questions take us no further but the open ones encourage the interviewee to wax lyrical.

Some other kinds of questions that can be helpful, especially if you want to make sure the interviewee repeats the anecdote they told you over the telephone when you were researching the interview, are those that begin: 'Tell me about...' This form of words encourages the interviewee to slip into storytelling mode.

Some professional interviewers think this kind of question is clumsy, but you don't need to worry about that. After all, you're not pretending to be a professional, you're simply after the best results you can get to explain the story of your enterprise. If you think the question itself sounds too clunky when you listen back, you can always edit the recording so that it's cut out and the interviewee appears to launch spontaneously into the anecdote that illustrates the point they were making before.

Good interviewers are also good listeners. You'll have made a list of questions but these will be only a guide. During the interview itself you shouldn't be rigid but allow the conversation to develop naturally. Don't be so busy sticking to your list of questions that you forget to pay attention to what the interviewee is saying. Be prepared to be flexible. Sometimes a completely new and fascinating line of questioning you hadn't previously thought of will spontaneously suggest itself during the interview, because of something the interviewee has just said.

KEEPING CONTROL OF THE INTERVIEW

As well as asking the right kind of questions to draw out the information you want, the best interviewers are masterful at using non-verbal techniques to encourage their interviewee. These will include:

- keeping strong eye contact;
- smiling;
- nodding;
- looking appropriately concerned when the interview takes a turn for the serious.

In other words, your face must express your encouragement and feedback so that the interviewee knows you are interested in what they are saying and you are responding as you're sure the people downloading the podcast will.

All of this has to be done without making a sound. Most first-time interviewers feel the urge to encourage their interviewees by murmuring 'yes, yes' or saying, 'mmm, mmm, uhuh, uhuh' but you will realize as soon as you listen back to the recorded interview that this is a ghastly mistake. What seems quite natural when you're participating in a conversation is extremely distracting and irritating when you're listening to one. Don't do it! It's very difficult to edit out these interruptions as they often cut across the interviewee's words. You'll want to scream 'shut up!' at yourself. Train yourself to do no more than nod silently whenever you feel the urge to agree.

As you become more practised and confident, you can also use these non-verbal techniques to steer the interview where you want it to go. If an interviewee is waffling on and on and should stop, try opening your mouth and drawing in a breath, as if you were about to interrupt. If you lift a finger as well, all but the most insensitive will draw their answer to a close! Leaning in towards the interviewee or straightening up and sitting back are both non-verbal signals that suggest to them whether they should keep talking or not.

My friend the professional interviewer explained how she often prompted the best answers without having to say a word. When the interviewee finished speaking, instead of jumping in with another question, the interviewer simply kept her eyes fixed on theirs and slightly raised her eyebrows. The interviewee invariably felt compelled to fill the silence and expand further on what they'd just said, often coming up with the most interesting material at that point.

AFTER THE INTERVIEW

When you've reached the end of the interview, check back over your list of questions to make sure you didn't miss anything out you'd intended to include. Sometimes you can find you were carried away listening to the answers, which is as it should be, so this is your opportunity to make certain that you have everything recorded that you might need for the podcast.

But don't be so obsessive about whether or not you've done the interviewer job properly that you forget to consider the feelings of your interviewee. Even the most friendly and light-hearted interviewing can be a gruelling process for both parties. It's especially tough on the interviewee, who has been asked to expose themself to the public gaze, sometimes revealing quite personal thoughts and opinions. The interviewee thinks of you, the interviewer, as the one in charge, the mummy or daddy of the interview, and imagines you have been in control throughout. They'll have wanted to please you by giving the right answers, but may be worried they've somehow failed to live up to your expectations.

Whatever you think about their performance, thank them for their time and trouble and assure them with all the sincerity you can muster that the interview was excellent and they did exactly what you wanted. Make them feel good about what has just taken place. Nine times out of ten, if you've done your job properly, the interview will indeed be marvellous, and it's only polite to show them how grateful you are. If it was terrible, dull and unusable, that almost certainly isn't their fault and why should you spoil their day over it? You chose the wrong person to talk to, or you asked the wrong questions. Later, in a week or two, you can let them down gently that you won't be using the material after all because... well, there was a technical error in the recording which you take full responsibility for, or the file became corrupted while you were uploading it to the website, and you had to find someone else instead to be interviewed in a hurry. Spread a little politeness in this dark world. It doesn't hurt to make people feel good when they've put themselves out for you.

Anyway, you may find the interview wasn't anything like as bad as you thought it was, and you can save it by some judicious editing. But that's the subject of the next chapter.

TOP TIPS FOR INTERVIEWS

Put time and effort into finding the right person to interview

Plan the interview in advance and know what the answers are you want from your interviewee

When you know the answers, then make a list of questions

Open questions, not closed: who, what, why, how or tell me about

Listen to the answers during the recording and be flexible

Keep eye contact and encourage your interviewee non-verbally

Don't say 'yes, yes' or 'mmm, mmm'

At the end of the interview check your list of questions to be sure you haven't missed any

Thank your interviewee afterwards

QUESTION

Do you know how to assess the voice of the person you are going to interview?

ACTION

With an audio interview you are not concerned with what your interviewee looks like, but how they sound. For your podcast you need to have someone who sounds warm and friendly and chatty, or has the authority to explain your product or service to those listening to the podcast. Most important, you need to find someone who can tell a good story. Try and talk to your interviewee on the phone before you book them for the interview – then you can listen to their voice and assess their value to your podcast.

CHAPTER 3
HOW TO RECORD YOUR PODCAST

PodioIndia

PodioIndia is an Indian music website which features songs, interviews and commentaries on a wide range of Indian music from Bollywood to classical. The podcasts are hosted by Piya and Deb Roy who interview musicians and singers and then include audio clips from their listeners who send in comments and original music. Deb grew up in Calcutta – that's in the Eastern part of India and his wife Piya comes from Darjeeling in the North East, and together they aim to podcast fresh voices, unheard compositions and new albums. The podcasts are free, but they have a business model that will take advertising. At present they are building their fan base worldwide.

The PodioIndia website which hosts the podcasts began in 2005 when Deb was discussing the new phenomena of podcasting with his wife over a cup of tea. They agreed it was a medium that they could develop as a home business. They decided to create podcasts about their personal enthusiasm for Indian music. Their podcasts would be different from any other because they would feature user-generated content such as comments about new albums, original music, or even cover versions of well known Bollywood songs. Within a year they were up and running and inviting people to share their love of Indian music at PodioIndia.

An important component of the website has been the quality of the audio recording. Deb says, 'We were a stickler for quality right from day one. We thought that audio where the listener will be using a headphone or earpiece has low tolerance for poor quality. So we were very, very fussy about quality.'

Deb and Piya bought a couple of high quality microphones, a mixer, and some studio grade software. Deb thinks that if you are creating a talk show for podcasting then you could get away with a less expensive microphone which plugs directly into a computer. But as PodioIndia was recording music he didn't want to lose nuances of the sound with poor audio production. Even with quality equipment his total expenditure on software and hardware was below the price of an inexpensive motorbike.

The second area that PodioIndia focused on was forward planning. Deb and Piya create what they call a 'show outline' that is not a detailed script but an outline of the order of programme contents. Even if they plan a free-wheeling conversation they have this outline script. First they make a list of what's going to be in the podcast:

- The contributions that they have received from listeners.

- The interview and its content.

- Music samples.

Then Deb and Piya create flash cards that outline the extempore conversation they'll have about the music. Everything is planned in advance of the recording. Since the podcast isn't streamed live, if they aren't happy with one segment of the show they'll record that segment again.

Initially contributors to the podcasts were friends and acquaintances of Deb and Piya who were interested in music. Although the first couple of episodes were made up of people they'd invited to contribute by e-mail, by the time the third episode was recorded they'd received contributions from lovers of Indian music from all over the world. A contributor from Russia once phoned them to say, 'I am an Azerbaijani but somehow I fell in love with Indian music and now I have made a career of singing Hindi songs in Moscow.' Since then, PodioIndia has set up a telephone number on which audio comments can be recorded for inclusion in the programmes. One of the podcast programmes is called 'Awaaz Anjane', in English 'The Voice of the Unknown.' It showcases the talents of people who haven't taken up music professionally. They perform either original music or cover versions of well-known songs. The podcasts are very popular, with more than 8,000 monthly downloads.

India is a land of unique diversity with many different languages and Indian music reflects the region from which it originates. PodioIndia has become the flagship for music programmes in Hindi, with 'Awaaz Anjane' joined by a second classical music podcast 'Alaap', but with Bengali being the fourth largest spoken language in the world Deb and Piya have created an affiliate web site called BanglaPodcast.com. Podcasts in Bengali promote Bengali culture globally. There's an Indian Conference that takes place in North America each year, and the podcasts help in event promotion and drive attendee registration.

PodioIndia is an exciting and creative business. Deb Roy has two pieces of relevant advice when it comes to recording audio. He says, 'Just because you are podcasting doesn't mean that you can ramble. Time is very, very scarce for people, you must respect the listeners' time. A five-minute show is sometimes better than a 50-minute show.' His second key point is about quality. Since many mainstream media companies are re-issuing programmes in podcast format you're competing with radio and television. 'The bare minimum that you have to do is ensure that yours at least is rival with the topmost audio quality.'

PLANNING NOT SPENDING

The temptation when you're planning your recording, particularly if you're the kind of person who likes gadgets and grown-up boys' toys, is to imagine that if you throw lots of money at the equipment you use for recording, the results will be all the more marvellous.

Not so. There's an old recording engineer's saying, 'rubbish in, rubbish out'. The best equipment in the world can't save your recording from sounding lousy if you don't know and apply the basic principles of recording audio. You'd be much better off with a cheap recording device set up properly, than a bells-and-whistles state-of-the-art studio gizmo in the hands of someone who hasn't the first clue how to use it. Anyway, if you had a vast budget to spend on your podcast you could afford to employ a professional sound recordist to do the lot for you, including supply of all the necessary equipment. But that wouldn't be nearly as much fun, would it?

The object of this book is, without blinding you with science, to teach you the secrets the professionals know, so you can see how easy it is to produce your own podcast. This chapter isn't going to tell you about what make or model of recording equipment to buy. That's a matter for you and your budget, and there are plenty of sources of information on the internet. Instead, it's going to explain the tricks recording engineers use to get the best possible sound quality out of their equipment. It's about where and how you place the stuff, rather than what format or what specification.

THE IMPORTANCE OF SOUND QUALITY

The first principle to grasp is that sound quality matters on a podcast. Why? Because people have to be able to hear it clearly. It mustn't be too loud nor too soft, and it mustn't be drowned out by extraneous and distracting noises. That means you're aiming for a crisp, clear recording without:

- distortion, which is what you can get sometimes if you use the equipment wrongly;
- muffling, which you might get if you put the microphone in the wrong place;
- excessive hollowness and echo, which can happen if you record in the wrong kind of room;
- irritating jumps in the sound levels so the person listening doesn't have to keep turning the volume up or down.

You don't have to turn out a piece of audio so perfect and crystal clear that you could hear a pin drop in the background. But you do want one that's free of crackle, hiss, static, popping noises, and unexplained noises off. All of these distractions and annoyances can make the difference between a podcast that people listen to, and one that after less than a minute they click off in exasperation. No matter how great the content, if people can't actually make out what's being said, there's no point.

So to record well, you need to use your ears – and use them in a way that's a little different from the way you usually use them, so that you can listen in the way a sound recordist does.

The technical bit

Broadly speaking, there are two types of recording equipment. On one side, old-style analogue devices, such as tape recorders and cassettes of various kinds, and on the other, more modern digital recorders. Analogue devices can largely be ruled out because, although there are still some of these around, glorious antiques lovingly cared for by those who swear they sound 'warmer' than digital, it's more complicated to transfer something recorded on one of these to digital form so it can be edited and uploaded to your website.

Digital recorders are easy to come by. Most don't use tape or discs, but are 'solid state' devices so that how much sound they can hold is determined by the amount of memory. They vary from basic Dictaphone-style devices that can be used for recording memos or conversations and meetings to be transcribed later, to more sophisticated machines capable of producing a sound quality good enough for broadcast. Some of these are remarkably small and lightweight, and not nearly as expensive as you might think. Of course if you go for the kind of models the BBC use for recording, you could pay a lot of money. But many small handheld recorders, primarily intended for business use, produce a sound good enough for podcast purposes. Most come with a USB connector to be plugged straight into your computer so you can easily upload the audio from them.

MICROPHONES MAKE MAGIC

A more important factor in the eventual sound quality you'll obtain is the kind of microphone you use. This is where it's worth spending a little extra money to achieve a remarkable leap in the sound quality.

There are many, many different types and makes of microphone on the market and it's impossible to do a proper comparison of their various merits here. But my advice would be not to settle for any 'basic' model that comes with the recording device and certainly **never**, **ever** use the built-in microphones that many recorders have. These are, without exception, poor quality not only because of their construction, but because it simply isn't physically possible to place them in the best spot for capturing a good, clear sound. A built-in microphone that's just about usable for dictation purposes won't produce a clear enough sound to be used in a podcast.

So allow some money in your equipment budget for a better quality microphone and make sure it's one that will plug in to your recording equipment. You can do this by buying it from the same source as the recorder and asking the person selling it to make sure it's compatible. Most recorders, even the ones with built in microphones, have a socket that will take an external mic. It doesn't have to be top of the range. Just a few extra pounds spent on a better mic can lift the sound quality by an extraordinary amount.

You might also find it useful to make sure your microphone comes with a small stand. In the movies, reporters thrust handheld microphones aggressively into the faces of their interviewees, but it's much more comfortable to set the microphone on a stand in the right spot so that you can forget about it during the recording and your interviewee is less conscious of its presence.

The other additional piece of equipment that can sometimes help is a pair of good headphones. Find a pair that sits comfortably on or in your ears and filter out as much external sound as possible. You might not actually wear these during the recording, but they come in useful to check the sound before and after.

BEFORE RECORDING

Before you use your recording equipment in earnest, take some time to practise with it and get to know it properly. You don't want to look like a fumbling idiot when you set it up in front of an interviewee – that would set the interview off on entirely the wrong foot. Also, you don't want to have to worry too much about whether or not the machine is recording when what you should really be concentrating on is the content of the interview.

Practising at home and listening back to what you record will teach you quite a bit about the way a microphone picks up sound, which is rather different from the way our ears usually hear it. Normally our brains filter out most irrelevant noise. Unfortunately microphones don't do that, they tend to emphasise it unless they're used properly. But provided you follow a few simple guidelines about how and where to record, it isn't too difficult to get the right sound for your podcast.

WHERE TO RECORD

The location you pick to record in can have a remarkable effect on the sound quality. The size and the shape of the room and what is on the floor and walls, all contribute to the overall sound. If these factors are within your control, it's worth taking time to pick the right sort of location so that you'll get the best possible sound. These apparently small factors can all combine to make quite a difference.

The problem is that in some rooms sound waves bounce around off the walls and collide with each other, creating some rather odd effects which colour the sound and make it more difficult for a listener to hear clearly. Big rooms can be very echoey, but some small rooms can sound strangely boxy, especially if they have too many hard surfaces, like a tiled bathroom.

Sound studios are specially designed to give what's called a 'neutral' acoustic. They tend to be smallish rooms with walls often padded or panelled with absorbent material to cut down on echoes and reflected sound within the room, as well as insulating it from outside noise. Even the tables in them are covered in fabric.

So, find a room to record in that's not too big and if you have to use a big room, sit in the corner rather than the middle. A low ceiling is better than a high one. Ideally the room should be carpeted, to absorb the sound waves. You might spread a cloth or a blanket over any hard surface like a table. If there are a lot of windows, keep them closed to cut down on noise from outdoors and draw the curtains.

You also need to make sure there are no distracting background noises. Before you do anything else, sit in the room, tell everyone in there with you to be quiet, and just listen.

What can you hear? You need to train yourself to notice all kinds of noises that you would normally ignore.

Is there a clock ticking? Turn it off or take it out of the room. If it really isn't moveable, think about finding a different room for your recording. Ticking clocks, normally just part of the background, sound abnormally loud and distracting on recording and they also make it harder to edit your finished recording.

Is there a hum in the room? Can you identify what it is? If it's a fridge, and they can be very noisy, turn it off. To make sure you turn it on again afterwards, put your car keys in there.

It might be a fish tank. To avoid the risk of slaughtering your host's prize collection of tropical fish, ask them if they would mind turning it off, and *write yourself a big reminder to turn it back on again*.

It might be air conditioning. This is less easy to turn off, especially in large office buildings, and you may have to live with it – but if so, try to position yourself for the recording in a part of the room where the noise is quietest.

Is there a television blaring in another room? Politely ask those watching it if it can be turned off, or at least if the sound can be turned down for as long as it takes to complete your recording.

SOUND SOLUTIONS

Closing the windows and pulling the curtains helps minimize noise from outside. There'll be nothing you can do about really thunderous traffic or rain on a tin roof, except wait for rush hour to end, or the rain to stop. In such cases the best strategy is usually to move to a different room, in a different part of the building away from the road or the source of the noise. But some outside noises can be controlled if you ask people politely to stop what they're doing for a short while.

'I've asked neighbours to stop mowing lawns, builders to stop hammering or drilling, even Mexican gardeners in Los Angeles to stop using their leaf blowers while I carried out a recording,' says Jenni Mills. 'Most people are happy to oblige if you approach them politely. Proffering a tenner to go and have a drink for half an hour could oil the wheels.

The only ones that defeated me were a team of bell ringers who refused to stop their weekly practice – and frankly, why should they? I couldn't blame them. I had to wait until they had finished before starting my interview.'

Why does it matter to remove as much background noise as possible? Because all these noises can be a distraction and make it harder for your listener to concentrate on the content of your podcast. Some, like aircraft passing overhead, will make it impossible to edit your interview if you need to, unless you want your recording to sound as if the plane has just dropped inexplicably out of the sky.

It's just as important to control 'noises off' if you are recording sound for video. If the picture shows a roaring log fire in the background, it doesn't matter so much that the microphone is picking up hissing and crackling from it. But if the people watching or listening to your podcast can't see the source of the noise they won't be able to identify what it is, and it could be very distracting.

Nowhere is perfect. Even some specially built sound studios suffer from underground trains rumbling beneath. You can become neurotic about eliminating even the slightest background whisper. The point is to do your best to listen out for and identify distracting noises, do something about them if you can, but accept that you can't always achieve the ideal acoustic.

In any case, where you place the microphone can help improve the sound even further.

WHERE TO PLACE THE MICROPHONE

Sound engineers often speak in reverent tones of a mysterious formula known as the 'signal-to-noise ratio'. This magic incantation determines whether you have a good quality audio, with crystal-clear speech, or whether the voices on the recording will be muffled, hissy, or otherwise drowned out by extraneous sound.

You needn't concern yourself with anything too technical, but it's useful to understand that the 'signal' is the part of the sound that you want the listener to hear easily, in other words, the voice on your podcast, and the 'noise' is all the other stuff that gets in the way – the background, in effect.

The closer you put the microphone to the source of the signal, with speech that's your interviewee's mouth, the more signal and the less noise. The further you put the mic away from the source of the signal, the more background noise.

Whoever is speaking needs the microphone to be reasonably close. How close? If you put it too close, you'll pick up a new kind of 'noise': irritating and distracting mouth noises, slurps and clicks and whistles to do with the movement of tongue and lips and teeth, which we don't normally hear because we usually don't place our ears right next to people's mouths.

Most recording devices, apart from the most professional types, look after the sound levels for you by using limiters and compressors that, in theory at least, smooth out the sound so you don't have to twiddle the knobs during the recording if there are unexpectedly loud or soft bits. However these can only help you so far; if you yell into a microphone very close to your mouth, the sound will distort and become unlistenable. By the same token, if you're whispering into a microphone placed too far away, the recorder can't cope and will raise all the background noise as well as the sound of the voice.

So the normal ideal distance for the microphone is not right up against a person's lips, but a comfortable 6 to 18 inches (15 to 45 centimetres) for most types of microphone. There are some very directional, focused types of microphone that work slightly differently from this, but it's unlikely you'll be working with one of these. Within that range, the microphone needs to be closest, at about 6 inches (15 centimetres) if there's a lot of background noise. If you were recording in a noisy pub or party you might move the mic even closer to the mouth, perhaps 4 inches (10 centimetres). If the room is quiet it can be at the further end of the range, but the further away you move it, the more you pick up what engineers simply call 'room', giving a sort of atmosphere to the recording which is made up of the reflected sound waves bouncing around the room. 'Room' isn't a bad thing until you get to the point, beyond 18 inches (45 centimetres), where there's so much atmosphere it makes the recording sound hissy and the voices muffled.

So as a general rule, make sure the mic is within that ideal range of distance, 6 to 18 inches, or 15 to 45 centimetres.

That applies to both voices in the interview of course, the interviewer's as well as the interviewee's. Even though the interviewee will be doing the majority of the speaking and their voice is the more important of the two, it would be irritating for the listener to have to keep twiddling the volume every time a question is asked because the interviewer is too far away from the microphone.

USING TWO MICROPHONES

There are two ways to achieve this. The first is to set the microphone in the middle between the interviewer and the interviewee, which is why a stand comes in useful. Make sure the microphone is pointing upwards and not pointing at one rather than the other, so it will pick up sound equally from both parties. If one of the two has a louder voice than the other you can compensate by moving the mic a little closer to the quieter person to favour them.

The alternative strategy is to use two microphones. You could either have two on separate stands each pointing at a person, or better still, when you buy your recording equipment, buy two 'lapel' mics, which are the kind of microphones most often used in television, tiny little devices that pin onto a collar or a tie or a lapel. In television the sound recordist goes to great lengths to conceal the wires by tucking them under clothing, but for an audio recording this needn't concern you.

Lapel mics are very easy to use, but make sure your recording equipment has enough inputs to connect both. Otherwise you can't go far wrong, as they're designed to be 'omnidirectional' and will even work if you accidentally pin them on upside down. Indeed it can sometimes actually help if you do this, should your interviewee be a man with wide flaring nostrils that make him a heavy breather.

The only drawback to lapel mics is that they can sometimes rub against clothing, producing loud rustling noises. So make sure you've pinned them where your interviewee can't dislodge them with wild expansive gestures, and persuade them to remove any scarves and jewellery. It goes without saying that you should have done the same before starting recording, whatever kind of microphones you will be using. Bracelets, especially, tend to click and jangle.

It's also a good idea for the people being recorded not to wear leather jackets, which creak alarmingly, and not to sit on leather sofas or chairs unless you wish your recording to be punctuated by what appear to be farts every time anyone moves.

Finally, it's not a good idea to handhold a microphone, whatever you may see on the movies. It's a sure-fire way of introducing more unwanted noise to your recording, because mic casings and cables are very sensitive and shouldn't be moved or handled during recording.

RECORDING OUT OF DOORS: A GREAT WAY TO ADD COLOUR TO YOUR PODCAST

Why would you want to record out of doors? Sometimes, the right background noise will enhance your podcast and make it much more lively and interesting. You can use background sound to help you paint a picture in the listener's mind. So, for instance, if you're talking to the farmer whose sheep produce wool for the knitwear you market, it will really add to your podcast to record out of doors in the meadow with a background of bleating lambs. But make sure it is background and the lambs don't monopolize the recording.

You might find it helpful to do a test recording first. This is always a good idea anyway, to check the equipment is working. For this, it could be worth investing in a pair of headphones, as it's easiest to judge the sound properly through headphones designed to cut out any extraneous noise. Again there are many different types on the market. Choose a pair that sit comfortably on your ears and that insulate you from as much background sound as possible.

Unless you have lapel mics, when recording out of doors you might have to use a handheld microphone if there's nowhere to balance a microphone stand. In such cases try to move the microphone as little as possible and certainly avoid letting the cable flap around or drag on the end that feeds into the microphone. That could easily damage the electrical connections and cause the mic to fail. Some professionals loop the cable round their hand to prevent this happening.

Hold the microphone between you and the interviewee, so that it will pick up both your voices. Although you want some background noise, you don't want it to predominate, so the ideal distance for the mic is about 12 inches (30 centimetres) from both your mouths, so you will have to stand quite close together.

One hazard of recording out of doors is wind noise. Because of the way microphones are constructed, instead of picking this up the way we hear it, as a pleasantly atmospheric whistling sound, wind on a microphone becomes a series of bangs and bumps. Even a light breeze can sound like a hammer thumping the microphone.

This can be minimized by putting a foam windshield over the microphone. Some, but not all, microphones come supplied with these, or they can be bought separately from specialist suppliers. If you don't have one, it's better to avoid recording out of doors on anything other than a still day.

Another useful trick is to use your body to shield the mic from the worst of the wind.

Although it's more difficult and the sound less easy to control, recording out of doors can often add something special to your podcast. Background noise, where appropriate, can bring a piece to life. The more you practise recording, the more sensitive your ears will become. You'll soon learn to identify the recording hazards, and create the right balance for the sound so that voices can be heard clearly.

AFTER THE RECORDING

Always check before you leave that your recording is there on the machine by listening back to a little of it. That could save you a wasted trip. But having listened back, be very careful before you record anything else that you are not going to record over the interview you've just completed and when you get back, transfer the material as quickly as possible to your computer ready for editing. It would be a shame after so much effort to lose the work you've done.

TOP TIPS FOR GETTING A PERFECT RECORDING

- Use a good microphone, not the built-in mic on the recording machine

- Get to know your equipment before you use it

- Pick the right place to record in: indoors, a smallish room with plenty of absorbent soft furnishings, outdoors, somewhere sheltered with background noise that is appropriate to the subject matter

- Before starting the recording, LISTEN for distracting or inappropriate background noise – ticking clocks, traffic, TVs etc

- Keep the microphone fairly close to the people who are speaking, and don't move it around

- Out of doors use a windshield

- After finishing the interview, check the recording before you leave

QUESTION

Have you practiced using your equipment?

ACTION

You can have the most expensive sound recording technology, but if you have forgotten to charge up the batteries or end up plugging the microphone into the jack plug for the headphones, then it is not going to work. You will look and feel foolish in front of your interviewees. Check your equipment and then check it again.

CHAPTER 4
HOW TO EDIT AUDIO

CASE STUDY

The Economist

The Economist is an authoritative weekly news magazine focusing on international politics and business news, edited in London and published on glossy paper. It has a growing circulation of about 1.6 million copies selling internationally. As well as world news, politics and business, *The Economist* covers books and arts, science and technology and publishes regular in-depth special reports including *Technology Quarterly*. The editorial is aimed at highly educated readers and it claims an audience of opinion formers and policy-makers.

But *The Economist* had a problem. It was a good problem, but it needed a solution. Like all magazines and newspapers, *The Economist* found that subscribers cited 'no time to read' in their top three reasons for subscription cancellation. Readers of *The Economist* are busy executives and are time poor. If you have ever taken a weekly subscription, it's easy to find a pile of magazines that you've read part of but never completed. *The Economist*'s digital strategy was very forward thinking in recognizing that offering an alternative digital platform in audio was complementary to both its online and print content. If you subscribe to the magazine you have access to the audio and you can listen to the sections you choose on your iPod or MP3 player as you drive to work, or when you are out on a run. The audio podcasting is a not a substitute for the print, but it augments the experience. The digital technology of podcasting allows for a weekly audio version of the magazine for people who are time poor but information hungry.

The Economist audio version is created by Jennifer Howard, MD of Talking Issues. She says that:

> *The majority of podcast listeners for* The Economist *come from the US, followed by Asia and Europe, and they say they listen to it in their car, on the train and in the gym, and they are getting through far more of the magazine than they would ever have time to read. A lot of people have said 'thank god for the audio edition, I would have cancelled my subscription otherwise'.*

Jennifer's company records between six-and-a-half to eight hours every week. She has a simple process. She records, which she says 'is the easy part', then she edits and then she has what she calls a 'proof listen' to ensure the material is accurate. With an international audience she knows that the pronunciation of names has to be perfect – and with 21 languages in any one week it's easy to make mistakes. If she's unable to track down the correct pronunciation of a personal name for example, at the very least Talking Issues ensures that the pronunciation across the article is consistent. The next step is a fine edit and then the audio is converted to both MP3 and M4a format at 48 kbps. Before the material is uploaded, Jennifer will tag the metadata with the article name, the selection name, the article number, and attach any artwork. Finally she'll code each podcast with the copyright details so that when it appears in the iTunes library or MP3 libraries the copyright is in place and the audio articles appear in the same order as the print edition.

Some weeks she is dealing with as many as 90 MP3 files in one zip folder and one six-and-a-half-hour M4a file. Then it is easy for the user to either download the one MP3 folder, or subscribe to an RSS feed which pushes the M4a file to the listener's iTunes library. Jennifer thinks it's important that the audio users can browse the material in exactly the same way as you browse a magazine.

Because Jennifer is creating six or seven hours every week she has considerable experience in how to record the material in the easiest and quickest way. It's her job to make sure that the audio version is ready to be downloaded before the print version is on the newsstands or delivered to the home of the subscriber. She says, 'What we do is practically live; we're reading printed material and recording it with as few mistakes as possible so that we have a one-and-a-half to one ratio when we edit.' Jennifer's advice is to create a paper edit as the recording is happening. She has the script in front of her and marks the place where there's a problem and an edit is needed. She says there are always problems. 'Tummy rumbles, script rustles, exclamations, coughing, not to mention stumbling over the international names!' She's convinced it's worth every effort to ensure the audio is as clear as possible, because quality is important to the user.

'Content and production quality is key to a good podcast. Nobody wants to listen to somebody recording in their bathroom'. Her results are professional and *The Economist* is downloaded by more than 60,000 people each week.

The first rule of editing is to back up every copy of the digital recording. As you work on the edit make sure you're creating backups of your podcast – you never know when you might have a power cut or computer virus.

The second exciting element of sound editing is that it's a visual as well as an audio skill. Sound editing equipment produces graphic representation of the sound waves, so you can see what you are editing, and some equipment will remove background noise and interference with one click.

EXCELLENT EDITING

The characteristics of a great editor are easy to identify but hard to find; spoken word editors are a rarity except in top recording studios or working at the BBC. Often the best sound editors are musicians because they have an excellent ear for cadence and pace; although they must be interested in speech and the spoken word. If your podcast is a disposable product, today's news and of no interest in a week, you'll be considering an edit ratio of 2:1. For something that aims to be the quality of an audio book, however, the ratio is more like 3:1 or more. When editing, in both cases you need to listen for mistakes and the loudest noises. Most podcasts will leave in minor little clicks or breathing because that's part of reality.

As a sound editor the most important area for you to concentrate on is clarity. Does what's being said make any sense? The sound editor will be listening for inflection, cadence, and pace in the voice, all of which should help make the recording clear to the listener. If you're going to have to pronounce tricky words then consistency is a key skill. When you've decided how to pronounce a word, then stick with that pronunciation for the complete podcast. Nobody gets the words correct every time and with a podcast you have a global audience that will e-mail you and tell you you haven't correctly pronounced the first name of the President of Azerbaijan! In the meanwhile, like Jennifer, as editor you will be cutting out any extraneous noises, breath, clicks.

Digital technology makes it simple to record material on your computer and share audio files with friends. You can record the material you require and then before creating a file to upload you can remove any noises you don't want. With the graphics of the sound on display you can see where to add the sound or make the edit. So you can synchronize music with speech or import new material and add it to your edit.

If you're self-producing, my advice is to have a couple of goes at recording the entire podcast without stopping and then take the best version. If there's something that was missed in the recording session you may need a re-take.

Don't worry if you make a mistake, it's easy to stumble on a word you think you know well, such as 'immeasurably'. It looks simple to say, but is easy to stutter over. Sometimes words just hit you, you just can't get past them and it's worth knowing there are good reasons why you'll have problems. Two consecutive vowels, or a long word that starts with a vowel, can disturb even the most professional actor. If you find you need three or four takes, use the beginning of take one up to the place where the audio is 'fluffed' and then use the best correct take following the fluff. So you might cut across from the middle of the sentence when you patch in the re-takes. If your original recording was at an unusual location with a noisy background, make sure you've recorded some 'atmosphere' as a background audio that you can use as background or space filler on difficult sound edits.

COVER UP YOUR MISTAKES

There's no question that it takes a while to learn to sound edit, but the basic concept is straightforward: take out what you don't like and cover up any other mistakes. Music creates atmosphere and can run under the recorded sound. If you need to hide a difficult edit you can increase the volume and that will distract the pod listener. Don't get carried away though with the power of music as your audience is really interested in hearing what you have to say. Music is an effect and should be balanced with the dialogue. Music creates punctuation to speech, it can be used to introduce different interviews or different emotions. More often it's used as an introduction and conclusion to each podcast. Sound effects are fun to add but it's a classic beginner's mistake to use excessive sound effects. You'll recognize a beginner's audio by the use of echo, reverb, and vibro effects. Don't show off, just concentrate on the story you're trying to tell. Sound effects can be a distraction from the words; ask a friend or colleague to give an honest opinion whether they work or not.

SOUND EFFECTS

Background effects are a less obvious editor's trick. They create mood and sense of place. Take your microphone to a range of different places and start recording your own background library. The beach in summer with seagulls shrieking and children laughing and the sound of waves breaking on the sand, or the shake and rattle of an approaching underground train. Most useful is the sound of the office; murmurs from meetings, the tip tap of the keyboard, the quiet ring of the phone. Of course you can buy CD's of sound effects, but recordings from your own business will be more convincing.

EDITING EQUIPMENT

Some editing software is available free. Free software is not just free of cost, as in 'free drinks'. It's free as in freedom, like 'free speech'. Free software gives you the freedom to use a programme, study how it works, improve it and share it with others. This free software is also called 'open source software', because the source code is available for anyone to study or use. There are thousands of free and open source programmes, including the Firefox web browser, the OpenOffice.org office suite and entire Linux-based operating systems such as Ubuntu. For more information, visit the Free Software Foundation.

An example of free software is Audacity, which was developed by a group of volunteers and distributed under the GNU General Public License (GPL). It's an easy-to-use audio editor and recorder for Windows, Mac OS X, GNU/Linux and other operating systems. You can use Audacity to:

- record live audio;
- convert tapes and records into digital recordings or CDs;
- edit Ogg Vorbis, MP3, WAV or AIFF sound files;
- cut, copy, splice or mix sounds together;
- change the speed or pitch of a recording.

Then there are sound editing packages that are free at a basic level but the manufacturers are convinced that when you start to use them you'll want to upgrade to a better level and they'll charge you for the additional effects and features.

An example of the free but you'll have to buy to upgrade is the WavePad Sound Editor audio editing software for PC & Windows, Mac OS X or Pocket PC. It claims its easy to use interface means you'll be able to start editing in just a few minutes. It allows you to record and edit music, voice and other audio recordings. When editing audio files you can cut, copy and paste parts of recordings then add effects like echo, amplification and noise reduction. The manufacturer's aim is that you'll want to upgrade and purchase a WavePad Master's Edition with audio restoration features including noise reduction and click pop removal.

There are also professional sound editing packages from international brands such as Sony and Phillips that are on sale at a medium price and claim they provide a complete professional digital audio production suite.

For those of you for whom the music on the podcast is going to be an important element of the pod experience then music orientated software such as the ProTools system has advanced music creation and production software and many new virtual instruments and plug-ins for music. If you're concentrating on talk then SADiE provides the tools for serious voice pod production and was created by experienced recording engineers. The SADiE sales spiel is that it can be used on location, or in a mobile truck, office, for multi-track editing, mixing, working to picture or in CD mastering. You will be surprised to hear that SADiE claims to have the slickest, fastest and most user-friendly interface!

If you browse the many different sound packages available on the market you'll see that many of them are without particular distinguishing features. You can buy them online. Then you download them or upload them onto your own laptop and you go from there. How long it takes to learn to use them depends on how good your technical skills are. You should be able to pick it up in a morning, longer if you're resistant to technology. It's not complicated, though.

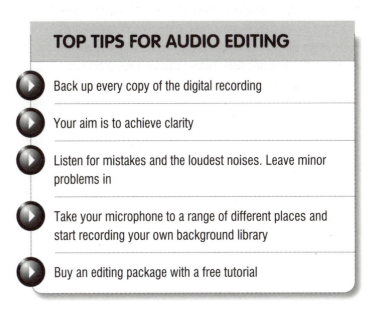

TOP TIPS FOR AUDIO EDITING

- Back up every copy of the digital recording

- Your aim is to achieve clarity

- Listen for mistakes and the loudest noises. Leave minor problems in

- Take your microphone to a range of different places and start recording your own background library

- Buy an editing package with a free tutorial

QUESTION

- Where is the back up of your recording?

ACTION

Do not start editing your audio before you have created a back up. Digital audio back ups are as simple to create as a saved copy of a word document. Unfortunately simple things are easy to forget. Create the back up and label it with the time and date. Then if you have any problems with your edit you can return to the original file.

PART II
VIDEO

CHAPTER 5
HOW TO RECORD YOUR VIDEO PODCAST

CASE STUDY

Lauren Luke make-up tutorials

Lauren Luke is a 27-year-old single mother from South Shields in the North of England who podcasts from her bedroom. She is a podcasting phenomenon. Her make-up tutorials have attracted more than 50 million hits on YouTube and, having signed up 250,000 subscribers in 70 countries, she has developed her own brand of make-up that sells online.

Lauren used to work as a taxi dispatcher where she was 'fed up with my job so I decided to start selling make-up on eBay'. At first she used a straightforward sales technique of showing the product in a photograph. Then she changed her approach.

'It's a bit boring to take photos of the product so I'd apply it to my eyes and experiment, take a photo, and then use that to show people what they could achieve'. She would use the latest colours on herself and post the results online. Within a short time the buyers started e-mailing her questions about how she applied the make-up in the photographs. The customers wanted specific product information, such as how to work with blue eyes or deep-set eyes. So Lauren decided to put video podcasts on YouTube that would show people her techniques, using the videos on YouTube to link back to the postings on eBay.

At the time she hadn't anticipated how desperate the cosmetic customers were to buy product from real people. Not all women feel like a supermodel in the product advertisements or want to be shown what to do with a product by one of those scary women in white coats who prowl the floors of grand department stores. Lauren's straightforward approach was a winner.

'I didn't expect what was to happen next; the visuals were really popular and views kept flying in – there was 100, 200, 300 saying please do celebrity looks and after-school looks – it just went from strength to strength'.

So how much podcasting expertise did Lauren have? It would be fair to say, none. She began with a USB webcam plugged into her computer with the camera perched on top of the computer screen web. It was cheap and she says, 'the quality wasn't so good. It had a blue tinge to it'. She would check the picture on her computer before she switched to record and because she was showing close-ups of her face she discovered that the lighting needed careful consideration. She placed a light behind the computer screen so that it shone directly on her face. She used an energy saving bulb, and removed the lamp fitting so that the light flooded her features. She spent some time getting the lighting correct.

'I used to mess about for ages and try to get the light right and I just found that a lamp stuck in front of my face worked. I looked a bit like a ghoul but you could see the colour.' She wasn't worried that in the background her bedroom was clearly in shot, complete with laundry and even her dog.

Her second key element was the sound. When she started, she used the microphone built into the computer. 'I remember it was fairly easy because I managed it so it wouldn't have been anything too technical.'

She has upgraded her camera twice – her first upgrade was to a digital stills camera that had a video setting. She used the USB point on the computer to download the videos. Lauren's podcast are 10 minutes in length and unfortunately the camera would cut off halfway through her recording. She bought new batteries and a new memory card, but the problem continued. Recently she has upgraded a second time to a hand-held video camera and there are no problems with the length of the recording.

Occasionally Lauren would use a title at the start of the podcast and still photos at the end to show the final look with close-ups of the eyes. She doesn't edit the material because she knows her viewers want to see what she's doing in real time. 'They want to see start to finish with no bits taken away.'

Now Lauren has her own website but she is consistent to her principle that customers will never feel intimidated. 'When you go shopping and you want to buy some make-up they make you feel bad, but now I'm trying to change the beauty industry and how people perceive it. Anybody can have fun and experiment'.

She always asks for feedback on every sale and she encourages people who have bought her range of make-up to make their own podcasts and show them online.

'It's something I want to know and I can actually put it right. I don't feel you get that kind of chance with the big cosmetic companies.'

Lauren represents the proof that a low-key business can be set up from a bedroom and that cosmetics do not have to be sold by supermodels or flawless beauties. Her videos show how to recreate make-up looks shown on TV from *Sex in the City* to Kylie Minogue. Podcasting from someone's bedroom has created a new line of make-up with worldwide sales.

Lauren Luke is a wonderful example of how to succeed with the simplest idea. You can be like her and just switch on the video camera and record what you do. But for the purposes of this chapter I'm going to assume you plan a little more. The key word here is plan. Before you start your video recording for your video podcast you need a plan. Write down what you're trying to achieve, what your final three minutes will be like when it's an edited, finished piece ready to upload online. Answer these questions. How long do you want it to be? What story are you telling? Who are you going to interview and what questions are you going to ask?

PLANNING: THE SHOOTING SCRIPT

The shooting script is a list of the shots you are planning to record in order to tell the story. As you are both the camera person and the director of your video podcast your list needs to be detailed.

It's impossible to have planned too much. Sort it out in your head and make yourself write it down. You can never entirely predict what's going to happen when you're shooting real people in authentic situations. Sometimes a noisy bit of machinery next door to where you're going to shoot means you've got to decamp to a totally different location. If you've written a shooting script it's much easier for you to think, 'Right, it will be okay if we go to this other location because the important things for me are listed on the shooting script and we can do that in this second location in the same way' or, 'we can't do it exactly the same way but this is how I'll alter it'.

If you went there thinking 'oh well, I'll just kind of play it by ear', when things have changed and they always do, then your video won't tell the story you originally wanted.

Your shooting script will have listed what you want your interviews to reveal. This will help when the person you believed was a fluent interviewee becomes completely tongue-tied or has a stammer or doesn't say what you'd planned. You have to check your script and think quickly on your feet as to how you're going to change things. 'OK, I'm not going to interview the managing director, we're going to do the sales manager instead.' Glance down at your script and ask yourself, 'what were the really important things that that interviewee was going to say?' Then ask the questions to get the answers from the sales manager.

SHOOTING ON LOCATION

Your shooting script will contain details of the location and what you're planning to shoot. Perhaps you were planning an outside location and it's raining. Because you've written down what the overall aim is you aren't going to shoot lots of shots of the orchard dripping with rain and looking awful because you thought you were going there to shoot the orchard. You weren't, your aim was that the location should look very rural. And you were using the orchard to do that. When you couldn't use the orchard, you swopped to something else. Your script helps you adapt when you're on location.

Finally you'll list the cutaways you're going to need, and how many. If it's essential to your story to get a good close-up of the goose eating, you wouldn't just shoot one and think, 'oh, that's fine I've got that'. You'd need to ensure you had three cutaways that you thought were good. When you get back and look at the footage on your computer, there'll be at least one of them that's not as good as you thought. Perhaps the interviewee moved too quickly or there was something in the background you didn't notice, like a plastic bag blowing about on the grass. You need to be covered for all eventualities.

Now you've finished planning you have a shooting script that lists:

- your aims and objectives;
- the interview – what will be said;
- the location – why it tells the story you want;
- the cutaways – what they add to the story.

FRAMING

The first thing you're going to think about when you switch the camera on, is framing. The biggest mistake with video podcasting is to shoot interviews too wide. If the interviewee is too small in frame they can't be seen. This is a beginner's mistake because camera wobbles show less on a wide shot, so it seems safer to use a wide frame. My advice is stay tight for a podcast. It works for Lauren Luke and her 50 million viewers and it will work well for you.

If you're doing a short interview and you're keen to focus on what the interviewee is saying you should set up a tight shot, the top of the frame being somewhere around the top of the head, cutting off the top bit of the hair, and the bottom of the frame being around about the collar bone. This, of course, depends on how good looking the interviewee is and also how harsh the light, but if they look reasonable it's a good trick for making sure the audience concentrate on the information.

Now if the interview is more than a couple of minutes long that can get a bit boring so now you want to change the shot.

CHANGING THE SHOT

When your interviewee isn't speaking, zoom out from the tight shot. Ask a question and then add, 'right, hold on until you answer because I'm just going to re-frame', then zoom out until you've got the top of their head in shot and the tops of their arms, cutting off the bottom of the frame around their chest.

The key here is to vary the interview between these two shots. You need the two shots to be appreciably different so the viewer's eye isn't jolted when you cut between the two.

THE ESTABLISHING SHOT

At the end of your interview, shoot an establishing shot so you can see the person in their surroundings.

Plan your establishing shots before you shoot your interview. It's often better not to shoot them until you've actually got the interview. Most ordinary people perform better on camera if you don't make too big a deal about the process, so place the microphone on them and start going almost before they're ready. Don't make them stand there rather nervously for ages while you check the shot. Then start with your two or three less important or crucial questions so that they warm up a bit. This is a good moment to collect information that you're probably not going to want in your finished interview. You might say, 'Tell me how long you've been in this business and what's been the most difficult thing about it?' It's hard to listen to the content at the same time as you're thinking about, 'is my shot okay?'

When you've completed the interview, you can confidently spend more time on the establishing shots. Ask yourself the question, 'What does the story need to tell? Why am I using this shot?' Now the story might be 'these animals are really well cared for'. In which case, you've got to see the interviewee walking along happily or looking happy being in the field with them. So you probably want several shots, some of which are really wide so you can see the animals grazing away happily, and some of which are close-ups.

A good tip is to start with a big close-up where the whole screen is filled with half of the cow's head. Choose something really big and dramatic. Then cut to a wide shot of that cow chomping away, grazing in the field. Then you might have a shot of the interviewee walking along, coming to the gate, resting on the gate. Then you'd cut to the interviewee in a close-up as they start to tell you their story.

AUDIO

The quality of your audio recording is even more crucial than the quality of the video. When you're shooting video you know that it's still usable if something is slightly out of focus or the camera wobbles a bit. If you can't hear what's being said you'll have to start again. It will irritate your viewer. If you have any doubt, re-read the start of Chapter 3, which tells you how to create the best audio for podcasts.

PLACING THE MICROPHONE

When you're recording an interview you need to have a separate microphone. The microphone fixed to the camera is not podcasting quality. It has been set up to compensate between the background noise and what someone is saying. When the speaker is quiet the background noise swells up. You'll be horrified when you play back the audio and it's unusable. You need to buy a small clip-on mic, and place it close to the interviewee's head, perhaps the jacket lapel or somewhere similar. Make sure no clothing will brush against the mic. There's a lot more detail about this in the earlier chapter on audio. It doesn't matter if the mic is in shot as most pod viewers feel they know the technology of recording and won't be surprised to see it.

LIGHTING

An expensive camera with an expensive lens will handle the contrast between bright and shady light. A less expensive camera will have problems. If you are shooting a head and shoulders with bright sky behind them, or with a white wall that's reflecting a great deal of light, it will create a contrast. On a cheap camera the contrast will make the person's head seem very dark. With the naked eye you won't see any contrast because your eye is better at compensating than a camera lens. So, the best light for videoing an interview is when it's a bit cloudy with soft overall light.

Indoor versus outdoor?

Modern cameras are excellent at recording using indoor light. But don't shoot your interviewee up against a window as the contrast between outdoor strong daylight and the indoor light will be too great and you'll have the dark head problem. You should be able to shoot most situations with natural light without having to 'light' it yourself.

If you have a reading light or a spot light you can bounce the light off a white wall onto someone's face. Bounced light tends to be flattering, but don't shine the light directly at the interviewee because it will make them squint. Look around the room and choose your interviewee's position carefully. The professionals' trick is to back-light. Out of shot place an anglepoise light which is shining directly onto the back of the head. It creates a halo effect of the light onto the hair so the subject stands out from the background.

CUTAWAY SHOTS

A cutaway shot enables you to edit your material. Imagine that you ask three questions and you want to use the first and the third one because the second was boring. You'll want to cut it out. You could just chop the first and third ones together, but it'd look jumpy. So you'd want to put a cutaway shot in the middle to hide where you're editing.

The aim of the cutaway is to create a bridge between the two shots. It enables you to tell the story without clunking jumps that hit the viewer in the eye. Of course there's a more informal style of shooting where the viewer is used to jumpy sequences and the camera moving around or where the camera swoops as if you were standing there and watching. Cutaways can, however, solve technical hitches in the edit so make sure you shoot lots of material.

Cutaways can solve the problem of changes in contrast. If you've got a dull day and then suddenly the sun comes out and changes the contrast the video will suddenly look too bright. If you're shooting a big movie, you down tools until the sun goes in again and restart when it's shady. If you don't have the time to waste, shoot a cutaway at the moment the light moves from cloudy to bright sun and from bright sun to cloudy so you could accommodate those changes.

USING A TRIPOD

Sometimes, as well as asking the questions, the interviewer wants to appear in the finished video. Now you have a choice. Either get somebody else to shoot for you, or put the camera on a tripod and frame the shot so that you are both in full view. The downside of the tripod is that you have a static shot. If your interview is longer than a minute and a half, stop and change the shot to a close-up of the inter-viewee. The upside is that the tripod keeps the camera completely steady, although this in turn can be a problem. When you edit material from something that's been shot on a tripod, to footage that's hand held, the material looks uncomfortable. Try to stick with hand-held shooting. It feels more immediate and informal.

MAKE-UP

Ordinary day make-up is fine for most podcasts, any heavy make-up will make the participants look unnatural. If your podcast is important to your business, you want it to be believable, credible and authentic so as genuinely to impart the information. Lauren has proved to all podcasters that natural is a good look. But bear in mind that the camera notices light more than a human eye. If light is bouncing off a shiny bald head, it will dominate the shot. Instead of listening to the message the viewer will be distracted by the shine. So, carry a little loose face powder and the problem is solved.

PROPS

There's a simple rule for props. If you need one prop, take several spares as well. Imagine you plan to shoot a scene of a girl feeding a horse an apple. You'll need more than one apple. By the time the microphone has fallen off, you forgot to remove the lens cap, you didn't manage to get the apple in shot and the sun went in, that greedy horse will have eaten four or five apples. You need enough props for several takes.

INTERVIEWING

Don't ask the same question twice

Assuming your interviewee is not an actor or a professional speaker, you'll discover that most people are very rarely better on 'take two' than they were on 'take one'. Most people take two or three questions to warm up when you're using a video to record them, so save your important question for after they've been talking for a minute or two. Listen carefully to the reply and make sure that it's not waffling on too much. Waffle is difficult to edit. My advice is to carry on, and then ask the same key question in a slightly different way. Your interviewee might say 'but you've already asked me that', and you just say 'tell me again'. If you say, 'Stop, your first explanation was too long – try and tell me shorter' your interviewee may become self-conscious and then go on in an unnatural style.

DE-CLUTTER

In the case study, Lauren chose not to de-clutter her bedroom and has made a feature of the normal everyday parts of her life that appear on camera. She's deliberately showing the beauty world her normal cluttered life. If you're planning a different story, though, you need to hold in your mind the idea that all the things that make somewhere look better to the naked eye work well on camera too. If you de-clutter before you shoot it's easier to notice what you've got in the background. So decide in advance if you want to show your laundry in the video. It's easy not to notice something in shot until you return to the edit and see that the cable from your camera is snaking around on the carpet. It hits you in the eye when you're editing on your computer but you didn't notice it at the time. Look carefully at all the different parts of your shot on your screen. Use the viewfinder and then look again without the viewfinder.

RATIO OF RECORDED TO EDITED MATERIAL

If you were making a professional television programme you might well expect to create four to five minutes of factual programme in a eight-hour day. For a podcast, you should try to avoid feeling over-rehearsed and lacking spontaneity. To be authentic you might need to move quickly, so assume at minimum a couple of hours. But first check out these common mistakes.

CLASSIC MISTAKES

Length

If your podcast is explaining something – try to be concise. Most people ramble when they speak. It seems fine when you're recording, but when you're editing it you'll be cursing yourself for everything being too long. Length is the biggest difference between material produced professionally for advertising and TV and amateurs 'having a go'. If you're the producer it's easy to overestimate the interest of your audience and the length of their attention span.

A good rule of thumb is that specialist information will command a longer attention span. For example, a teenage girl passionate about ponies will watch an information video on a website about horse riding for 20 minutes. What's more she'll concentrate and watch how the ponies are ridden. Compare that with an advertisement on television where the entire story is told in 30 seconds. Don't be self-indulgent. Don't draw things out too much.

The curse of the boss

If you're the Managing Director of a company you might think you've got something really important to tell your staff in your podcast. Think what you've got to say, say it to yourself and then ruthlessly make yourself say it in half the time. I suppose if your staff are paid to listen, then you can keep going all day, but if you want them to be interested and entertained, be snappy. If it's a message that is going to be seen by clients, remember they won't be so willing to be bored.

If you're producing a video podcast for the MD don't invite the sack by announcing, 'Look, you're being boring, do it quicker'. Try saying, 'that was marvellous, fantastic, brilliant. Now just go over that again but we've got to be really concise. This time let's just try to get point A and point B across and forget everything else'.

Most viewers have a short attention span. When you've had the problems that the edit suite throws up, you'll be sitting there thinking, why didn't I do that again? Why didn't I make that shorter?

Written piece to camera

If you are determined to read as you face the camera, it had better be interesting. It's better to appear, as Lauren does in her make-up podcasts, as if you're just talking to people directly. Even if you stumble a bit or don't get your words exactly right it's nearly always more interesting than reading something. If you have some important figures that you need to read aloud, you'll need to top and tail the reading with a section where you were just genuinely looking into the camera and speaking to people off the cuff.

Look into the camera

Look 'down the lens'. If you look slightly off you look shifty and untrustworthy. If you pin up a script beside the camera and your eyes are sliding across and refocusing slightly when you read, you'll come across as untrustworthy. Try to sit still. The most common nightmare is to have someone on a swivel chair moving from side to side as they talk. You barely notice when you're actually in the room and interviewing, but the camera picks it up. Editing, you'll be kicking yourself and saying, 'why didn't I tell him not to swivel his chair?' 'Why didn't I make them stay still; how could I not have noticed that?' The camera picks up mannerisms more than the human eye does.

Slow pans

Panning shots, where you are moving the camera sideways or up and down, are nearly always too slow. Imagine you had a cottage for rent. You wanted to show that the cottage was near the sea so you shoot the sea and then you do a 20-second pan across onto the cottage. That's too long. It's boring when you're watching it on screen. Keep doing the same shot again and again, each one faster than before. When you've done one that's so fast you say to yourself, 'that's far too fast, nobody will be even to tell what's happening', that's the shot you'll use in the edit.

One-shot action

It's much harder than you think to do one shot that has lots of different action. It is great fun to try, but hard to pull off, especially if you want to do something that depends on separate bits of action all happening within the same shot. It takes time, careful planning, and a team who can remain natural doing the same thing again and again.

Use of zoom

Avoid zooming in shot unless for comic effect or a 'crash zoom' from one object to another. You're better off without it.

TOP TIPS FOR VIDEO RECORDING

▶ Have a plan

▶ Include plans for the interview, location and cutaways

▶ The quality of the audio is more important than the pictures

▶ Use a tight shot

▶ Don't ask the same question twice

▶ Don't record too much

QUESTION

Where is your written plan?

ACTION

Just because you are creating a video doesn't mean that you don't have to write anything. In fact the written plan is the most important element of your video podcast. You need to create a shooting script, and for that you need a clear written idea of what the podcast is going to be about. Don't switch the camera on before you have planned your shooting script.

CHAPTER 6
HOW TO EDIT YOUR PODCAST

CASE STUDY

Ben Brownlee – Curious Turtle Editing

Ben Brownlee has been an editor for over a decade. He runs his own business, Curious Turtle, from his home in Denmark. Primarily a training company offering courses in the most popular video editing applications, Curious Turtle also accepts editing contracts from a range of clients, both for broadcast and for the web.

Ben has found that web-based projects, whether viral advertising snippets, video podcasts or corporate identity promotional videos, have been on an upward curve for a while:

The advent of faster broadband connections has meant that more and more companies are incorporating video into their web presence. It's now possible to present genuinely good quality video on the web, which hasn't been the case until relatively recently.

Faster internet access allows Ben to perform his editing remotely and costs have been significantly lowered, with no need for expensive shipping of tapes back and forth. 'Client approval videos are sent by e-mail, changes are returned by e-mail and the final edit is delivered either completely digitally onto an ftp site or mastered onto a DVD.'

Yet while faster access, greater bandwidth and an increasingly computer-literate world have all helped Curious Turtle to flourish, familiar problems continue to surface associated with the editing process:

As an editor, I'm often not involved in the early stages of a project. Someone else has planned and shot the material and it's my job to shape it into something that tells the client's story and that shows their business in a positive light. The material I receive has often been shot by someone without a great deal of experience. Too much footage is a common problem in such cases, but, while time-consuming, it doesn't hinder the editing process as much as not shooting the right kind of material.

Ben recently edited a short, four-minute video for an architectural firm with the aim of providing a corporate profile made up of shots of their offices, details of some of their projects and standard to-camera interviews. It was a simple project aimed at bringing their architectural achievements to life without relying on pages of text and standard still images. Unfortunately, Ben's task turned out to be far from simple.

The first issue concerned the location of the interviews. Recorded in the offices themselves, scant attention had been paid to the setting and the background was full of clutter and office paraphernalia. Ben remembers:

It was far too distracting There were too many elements in the shot that simply did not belong in a nice, sleek presentation. On top of that, the camera was static at all times, which meant it was difficult to make a clean edit when trying, for example, to match the beginning of one sentence with the end of another.

To remedy the situation, Ben took advantage of a funda-
mental difference between creating video for the web and for
television:

> *The size of the picture for the web is small, so it's possible
> to crop footage without sacrificing the quality of the image
> itself. It's not a perfect solution, but in this case I used
> a cropping and scaling technique to remove much of the
> background to ensure that the viewer's focus remained
> on the interviewee.*

> *The cropping also served a second purpose of allowing
> me to create the illusion of camera movement. When I cut
> between different sections of a particular interview, the edit
> did not jar with the viewer because I was able to cut from
> a wider shot to what appeared to be a close-up. It
> improved the flow and made it appear more dynamic than
> a long, static interview, despite the content being
> essentially the same.*

A second problem was an irritating hum from a microphone that
plagued the entire recording:

> *There are a few different ways of dealing with sound issues,
> but on this occasion I employed a noise reduction
> technique. Basically, the software analyses a sample of
> the hum and is then able to return to the footage and
> reduce those frequencies. Although it may not eliminate
> the hum completely, it can drastically improve the quality
> of the sound.*

Finally, Ben was left with a more delicate concern. The main
interviewees had all been asked to think carefully about what
they wanted to say and to distil it into small chunks where
possible. The reason was two-fold. Because of the immediate
nature of the internet and the ability everyone has of navigating

away from a page with a single click, it's vital to grab attention and get a message across without boring the viewer. Secondly, and especially if it's a video that might be watched by a large number of people, there are issues surrounding server costs. Long videos usually result in a poorer quality of image.

Even so, several of the interviewees spoke for over 25 minutes each. While Ben knew there were ways of cutting the interviews down effectively, he had to guard against potentially causing offence to those who were, after all, paying for his services.

His solution involved some clever diplomacy:

What I did was to present them with two final versions. The first was, to be blunt, something approaching a wall of sound with the interviewees talking for far too long. The second was a similar edit offering the same message, except I had removed the material that I felt was redundant.

I was able to lead them towards the shorter, more concise version that I knew would work far better for the web, but the choice was still theirs.

Ben allowed his clients to become part of the editing process and to feel like they had made the decision to reduce their personal content for the good of the video overall:

In the end, what it comes down to is either making a shorter video that looks better or making a longer video with a lower image quality because it needs more compression. What we arrived at together was a sharp, clean, fresh piece of material that the client was happy with, which is really the most important thing!

In this chapter I'll explain how it's possible for anyone to edit their own video podcast cheaply and to a good standard. As with any technology, it's possible to spend extra money to produce ever more impressive pieces of work, but cost need not be a factor and previous editing experience is not a prerequisite for creating an attractive, effective video for your website.

GETTING STARTED – SOFTWARE

Most home computers manufactured in the last few years are capable of editing video with no problems at all. In fact, PCs and Macs usually come with free editing software, Windows Movie Maker and iMovie, respectively. If you don't have either of these programmes you can download them from the web, but feel free to browse other no-fee alternatives such as Jump Cut, Jahshaka or VideoSpin.

Programmes such as Movie Maker and iMovie make it easy to transfer material from a standard DV camera to your computer. From there you can make basic edits to produce your video and export it to a format suitable for playing online, or onto a DVD that you can pass around to friends or clients.

These programmes are specifically designed for people without editing experience, so if you have made a careful plan of your shoot and have a clear idea of what you want to achieve, then they are perfectly adequate tools for creating a decent standard of content.

Naturally, free software is limited in comparison with more professional programmes. Really fine editing is not possible, so be prepared for the fact that you'll be more reliant on longer shots rather than MTV-style fast-paced cuts. This isn't necessarily a drawback, though, especially if you're just starting out. The temptation to indulge in all the flashy aspects of a more complicated editing programme can have a detrimental effect on any project.

Free software wouldn't have been sufficient to produce the kind of sleek, professional video Ben Brownlee delivered to the architectural firm in our case study. The limitations regarding the number of cuts and the quality of edits along with a reduced freedom to use music and alter the audio would have made his task impossible. Yet basic software doesn't have to result in an inferior video. If you consider how to convey your message in the simplest way, without relying on fancy editing techniques, you can create a video that would look at home on the most modern of websites. This kind of software may not be perfect, but it allows you to import images and graphics and its very simplicity will force you to focus on sharp, absorbing content.

UPGRADING YOUR SOFTWARE

If you believe that your project needs more precise editing than free software can offer, or perhaps having shot and edited a few successful video podcasts of your own you feel you are ready to move to the next level, then there are a variety of programmes you can purchase. They won't guarantee that your video will be better than one produced by free software, but they will open up new doors and offer you the chance to raise your ambitions.

For Windows, a popular solution is Adobe Premier while for the Mac a decent place to start is Final Cut Express. Be aware that these and similar products are not something you can grab and intuitively pick up in a few minutes, but at the same time there are manuals and online tutorials that can help you. Many companies, such as Curious Turtle, offer more intensive courses and inexpensive DVD training programmes that can have you up and running within a few hours.

The decision on whether to invest in this software comes down to the kind of video you want to produce and the amount of time you can commit to your project. If it's fairly uncomplicated, perhaps using interviews, graphics and some music, it's perfectly possible for anyone to learn how to use such software with relative ease. If you want to go further, to immerse yourself in the craft of editing, then it's worth considering professional instruction.

SELECTING YOUR MATERIAL

Once you've shot your material and feel you're capable with whatever editing software you've decided to use, you're ready to start shaping your video. In fact, thinking of the editing process as crafting a sculpture is a useful metaphor.

The first thing to do is select the 'stones' you want to use. At this stage you're searching for the basic building blocks of your sculpture. Start by watching the footage and when you think you've seen something useful, transfer it from your camera to your computer, giving yourself plenty of leeway either side of the section. There's a definite balance to be struck here; don't limit your choices by rejecting too much material, but at the same time don't confuse yourself by transferring too much and wasting disk space at the same time.

Keep in mind how long you expect the final video to last and use it as a reference point. Of course, much depends on how much material is available, but, as we saw with Ben's project, you could be faced with a couple of hours of footage that needs to be whittled down to a mere four minutes. In a case like that, this rough pre-edit should see you eliminate an hour or more of the material.

SHAPING YOUR MATERIAL

The second stage is to begin shaping the outline of your sculpture, to start forming the broad basis of the story you're trying to tell. Whether it's for a feature film, a 30-minute comedy or a four-minute promotional video, you're always telling a story. It sounds almost too simple, but start looking for your beginning, middle and end. Remember you want to create an engaging video, not just a random collection of scenes or interviews. Poor editing can make even brilliant footage look tame, but in contrast, clever, vibrant editing can render the most mundane subjects interesting.

Work quickly here. Watch the footage, drop the sections you like into your timeline and move on. This is one of the most creative moments of the process so don't get waylaid by details; just keep those creative juices flowing. Don't worry too much about how it looks and feels at this stage, all you're looking for is an overall shape.

APPLYING THE DETAIL

If we imagine that your final video is aimed at being four minutes long, you should now be left with about eight or nine minutes of material. Before you do anything else, watch what you have and you'll notice that some sections will seem too long and others will seem out of place or redundant. Having established the shape of your sculpture, it's time to use your finer tools to craft some detail.

You may find that sections that seemed perfect now appear out of place. Be brave and remove them or relocate them to another part of your story. Remember that nothing is locked down; you can always reinstate pieces of footage later if you wish.

To craft your final version you'll now start to smooth over your edits by utilizing cutaways, or covering shots, to improve the flow. If we return to the Curious Turtle example, Ben shrank large amounts of interview footage down to just a few minutes while still maintaining the course of the story. When you reach this stage, a good tip is to concentrate on the sound rather than the pictures. Pick up the three or four sentences that you want to link together to make your point and place them together on your timeline. You'll be left with a soundtrack that makes sense, although the pictures will be jumpy and untidy.

For his video, Ben used a range of cutaways to cover these edits, including images of architecture and general office footage. Your cutaways will depend on your subject, but the important thing is to remember your story. Keep the cutaways relevant to what the interviewee is talking about and make sure they reflect where your story is heading. Cutaways can be as simple as a gesticulating hand that emphasises a point or a carefully placed image that illustrates the product or service being discussed.

THE FINISHED PRODUCT

When you believe your video is near completion, stop work altogether and take a break. If you can sleep on it then so much the better, but if you are pressed for time then walk away for at least half an hour.

Editing is an intensive process and it can be easy to become blind to any potential problems. A proper break will create some distance between yourself and the video and give you fresh eyes next time you look at it. When you return to the material you will need to be critical of your own work and be ruthless enough to remove any section that isn't contributing properly to the overall piece.

Think about what you're trying to achieve with your video podcast. If you're marketing a new product, have you explained why your product is better than or different from everything else on the market? Have you kept faith with your original objective? Make sure everything in your video genuinely enhances the progression of the story.

This isn't about equipment; it's about content. There are many videos online that have long, boring sections that drag on without having a point, or videos that are full of dead air and dead space. Keep yours concise and compact because it's so easy for people to click away to a competitor who's more adept at holding their attention.

There's a law of diminishing returns when it comes to honing and attempting to perfect your video, so draw a line and stop or you'll drive yourself mad. Show it to a friend. Question them about it. Is the message clear? Did any section feel too long? Would they have liked more information about a certain aspect?

Editing is an intensely personal process and objectivity can be difficult to achieve, but while it's important to consider all criticism, don't abandon your ego altogether. If you really believe in something you must fight for it, just be sure you know why.

COMMON PROBLEMS AND HOW TO DEAL WITH THEM

Buzzing or humming on the soundtrack

In our case study, Ben dealt with a faulty microphone by using a noise reduction filter. This is undoubtedly an effective method that's possible with more advanced editing suites, but there are other ways of fixing sound problems.

First, any kind of speech often forces more mundane noises into the background because viewers are listening to what's being said. That means a buzz is often only an issue when no one's talking. In this case, simply turn the sound down for a few seconds between speeches and the buzz will 'miraculously' seem to disappear.

Second, a continuous music soundtrack can divert a viewer's attention from any possible hum. The use of music could have a separate beneficial effect of craftily shielding a slightly dodgy edit as well. The art of cutting is about not jolting the viewer and continuous music helps to smooth the passage.

Uncomfortable interviewees

It's extremely obvious to any viewer when an interviewee feels uncomfortable in front of the camera. Even if the words make perfect sense the viewer may be distracted by darting eyes or fidgety hands and the message can easily be lost.

If you're faced with such a dilemma then you need to utilize your cutaways. Take a brief moment to establish who is talking and then try to cover their discomfort by using their speech as narration over other footage or images. Always be sure to follow their thought processes though, and make sure your cutaways are relevant to what's being said.

Remembering your medium

Always keep in mind that people will not be viewing your video podcast on their 40-inch widescreen HD TV. There are numerous examples online where this has been forgotten and as a result shots are too wide and the main subject too small. If you are faced with this problem, try Ben's method of cropping the image to place the subject firmly in the foreground.

It might be fun to make lots of flashy cuts and try to create an MTV-style effect to your video, but for the web this isn't very effective. Because of the limitations of final compressions, changing shots every second really only means that the picture quality of your video will be reduced. Rein in your wildest ambitions. Higher quality can be achieved through greater simplicity.

Another common problem with online videos is a lack of focus. If you can make your point in three minutes, do it. Your seven-minute version may look prettier, but people will grow bored and tune out if they're not receiving new information.

Don't make edits just for the sake of it. Have a browse online and you'll come across videos that cut with metronomic precision every four seconds for no discernible reason. The effect of this can be hypnotic and the rhythm becomes boring, so mix up your edits, keep it interesting and make sure every edit has a point.

Special effects

It may be tempting, but keep your fingers away from those special effects. As much as they may seem fun and new to you, the fact is that everyone has seen most special effects before and you run the risk of producing an amateurish piece of work.

A grammar of editing has been built up over many years. If you're determined to use an unusual transition, make sure it has a point, such as using a clock-wipe to indicate a passage of time. Ninety-five per cent of your edits will be straightforward cuts or cross-fades, ideal for a transition to a new location or subject, and if you keep that in mind you shouldn't go too far wrong.

TOP TIPS FOR VIDEO EDITING

- Free software may have limitations, but use this as a positive to create a simple but effective video

- Plan the story you want to tell in advance and always keep it in mind

- When beginning the edit, don't get bogged down in small details

- Keep your cutaways relevant and ensure they reflect the story you want to tell

- When you think you have finished, take a break. You'll return to your work with fresh objectivity

- Ask a friend to give their thoughts on your video

- Don't be too ambitious. Simplicity and clarity is key to a successful online video

- Make sure every edit has a point

QUESTION

Before you start your edit, do you know how long you want the final video to last?

ACTION

Your final video podcast will depend on how much material is useful. If you are a beginner you will probably have shot much more material than you can use – so decide how long the podcast is going to be and then create a 'rough cut' which may not be perfect but will help you eliminate material and save time in the editing process.

PART III
AUDIO AND VIDEO

CHAPTER 7
HOW TO UPLOAD YOUR PODCAST

Uploading and server technology

Earlier in this book there is a case study from Jennifer Howard and her company, Talking Issues, who successfully record and edit podcasts for *The Economist*. She makes it sound trouble free. However, her company almost went out of business when her server crashed and she was told that the cost of new technology was more than she could possibly afford.

When Jennifer set up the Talking Issues website for the audio versions of *The Economist*, she discussed her requirements with the computer team who cabled her offices. They agreed to set up a computer server for the podcasts. The computer team needed clear information about how many downloads of *The Economist* would take place each week. Jennifer didn't know. It was a new service. It might be popular, but then again how could she be certain how many people would download the podcast?

She considered for a while, and with help from *The Economist* management team replied, 'Let's assume we're going to get 50,000 downloads a week'. So her computer team set up a server and space from a network in East London and the service went live. In the first week *The Economist* had 12,000 downloads, in week two the number had increased to about 15,000. But in week three the server crashed. Not because she had more than the 50,000 downloads she had specified, she'd actually had 60,000, still within the capacity of the server to handle. But because she had 60,000 *concurrent* downloads.

The Economist isn't a service where people download the audio from time to time across the week. Readers want to hear the audio the very moment it's available. So when *The Economist* readers in New York get out of bed in the morning and go online, they download the podcast. Then the readers in Chicago go online and start their downloads. Then Los Angeles comes online and then Buenos Aires, and on it goes around the globe, huge numbers of people all downloading at the same time and crashing the server with requests. Jennifer had four days to sort the crisis before the next week's edition was going to be live on the site.

She asked her friendly local company to create a solution. She remembers:

> *They did a lot of teeth sucking and heavy sighing. Then they spec'd us a whole rack of servers. Their plan was that as more people came on line around the world then a new server was available. Unfortunately that was going to cost us £900,000. We might as well have shut the doors right then. Our business was finished before we had started.*

Jennifer desperately needed an alternative.

Fortunately, another IT expert suggested an international cache system. Now Jennifer uses a company called Cache Fly.

This is a content delivery network provider that relies on routing the material rather than holding it in a fixed place. So if you are in Chicago, the material diverts to the Chicago server. If you are in Paris it diverts to the Paris server. It eliminates waiting time and rather than 'hosting' the material, the system focuses on delivering.

The learning from her story is that the host or server capacity where you're placing your podcast needs to be sufficient to meet your users' needs. This chapter shows you how to plan ahead.

The whole point of creating a podcast is so that people can listen to it on their mobile, or on their computer. Most mobiles support MP3 and MP4 files, so that is what you're going to be creating for your users.

THE WAV FILE

When you've made your recording you'll have created your podcast as a digital Wav file which is saved at 705 kilobits per second. You can put this Wav file directly onto a disc or CD or, of course, keep it on your computer. To make the file suitable to go on your website or onto iTunes to be down-loaded you'll have to convert the file to a new format called MP3. Before you upload your podcast you need to convert it to a smaller size of 48 bits per second. You're going to squash the file and remove some of the audio detail to make it quicker to upload and download. All the bits above and below the recorded level will be compressed and squashed. For voice quality this isn't a noticeable differ-ence, it's usually only sound engineers who can identify a compressed voice audio. However, with music, which has a broader aspect, you don't want to squash the sound and compress the top and bottom notes, so if you're going to podcast your music you might want to consider using a larger file size.

But for the moment let's stay with your mainly speech-based audio or video recording. I'll assume you've completed the editing and checked that the sound levels are at a good quality throughout. Now there are two technical terms you need to know:

- render;
- convert.

Rendering

First you need to render all the different tracks into one final piece. Your Wav file is made up of the different tracks and when rendered they'll be pushed into one track, a mix of everything you've added to the podcast.

Converting

Then your audio needs to be converted from the Wav into a squashed podcast file that is easy to upload and download. Here you have choice as to the size of the file: 42 kilobits per second is the quickest to download but not the best in terms of sound quality, 128 kbps is preferable, but will be slower. At present most users will be familiar with the MP3 files, but the latest technology is an MP4a file, which uses less space, is quicker to download and is of higher quality. It's not difficult to predict that it will overtake MP3 in the future. Probably the way to go if you want to future-proof your business.

IT'S EASIER THAN YOU MIGHT THINK

Converting software is simple to use. Open the software and a window appears. Drag the Wav file into the window. Choose the folder where you'd like the converted file to end up and click Convert. Then your MP3 file is in the folder ready to upload.

The good news is you can find free conversion tools on line. The Switch Sound file converter is easy to master, and there are many others available. However, you might want to consider buying conversion technology. If you make a purchase, then you will get technical back-up support in terms of warranties and training which will help should things go wrong. If you've spent hours creating your podcast you don't want to lose the file. So the choice of pay or free is up to you.

Sometimes there are problems with converting files. This is a check list for fixing problems with your file conversions:

- Check the file is where you left it has and hasn't been removed.

- Check the file is not corrupt; if it is the converter cannot recognize the coding.

- Check the file size. If the conversion fails your file size is probably too large for the free software you're using. You might need to sign up for a more sophisticated converter.

Now your converted material is ready to upload, where do you plan to publish it?

If you don't already have a website with a URL, the appendix tells you how to do this.

Now there are many different ways you can publish your podcast. To make this easy I'm dividing your options into two choices: very quick, and a bit slower.

VERY QUICK UPLOADING

Uploading to specialist podcast sites for free

Perhaps the best-known podcast site is iTunes, but there are also many others. Type **podcast hosting** into your search engine. It will provide you with the most up-to-date list. Use the one that's most appropriate for your content. These companies will not only store your podcasts, so you don't actually have to own a website, but will also give you information about how many people have downloaded it. If you want to link to the pod from your website then, when you upload your podcast, you'll need to create a link from your site to the pod. So you need to make sure the podcast has metadata attached to it. Pretty simple. Before you hit the publish button just make sure your podcast has:

- a name or title;
- an episode number and description;
- the link to your MP3 file;
- any other key words that will help Google or other search engines find your podcast.

HOW TO ADD YOUR PODCAST TO THE iTUNES WEBSITE

1 Open the iTunes programme.

2 Sign-in to the iTunes Store and create an account. If you don't have an iTunes account, click on the button on the top right that reads **Sign in**. Create your account and make sure you're logged in.

3 Within the Store, click on the **Podcasts** section which brings you to the podcast directory.

4 Click **Submit a Podcast**.

5 Enter your podcast feed URL. Do this by copy and paste so you don't make a mistake.

6 Click **Continue** and iTunes offers a new screen for you to fill in with information in order to tag the podcast, eg the language it is recorded in, the category it falls under.

7 Click both **Confirm** and **Submit** and wait for the e-mail saying your podcast has been accepted.

A bit slower uploading

If you already have your own website and URL, and that's where you want to put your podcast, you need to work out if you have enough storage space to hold your pod, and just as important if you have enough space for users to come to the site and download the pod. I suggest you go back and read the Talking Issues case study.

Return to your hosting company and check that they have room for the audio podcast; most of them allow for one gigabyte of storage. So if you're planning a series of podcasts this is the moment to work out how much space they're going to need on your site. Ask yourself these questions:

● What length, in minutes, is each MP3 audio?

● Is the file 42 kilobits or 129 kbps per second?

● How many episodes are you planning?

● How many episodes will you have available at any one time?

A simple rule of thumb is to multiply the answer to the first question by the size of the file (42 or 129) to find out how big your files are going to be and then again by the number of episodes to find out how much storage you need.

Now you need to work out if lots of people are going to download at the same time, like the problem they had for *The Economist*. Here you need to know what's called 'the bandwidth figure', the size of the podcast files multiplied by the number of people who will be downloading it at any one time. Like Jennifer, you can't know this until you have started podcasting, but make a guess and tell your hosting company; you can always increase the hosting space at a later date.

REALLY SIMPLE SYNDICATION

You'll also want to create an RSS feed so your users can have an automatic checking system that lets them know you've updated the site. RSS feeds are useful for all updating, eg blog entries, news headlines, both audio, and video, and use a standardized format. Your website users will tell the RSS reader they want to receive your updated podcasts. Then the podcast is sent to them and can be read by using software called an RSS reader. Your podcast user will have the RSS reader either on the desktop computer or on the mobile. Your podcast user subscribes to your service by entering into the reader your URL or by clicking an RSS icon in a browser.

RSS feeds are available free; the free feeds are fine for someone who isn't doing lots of podcasts. However, it won't give you subscriber and download statistics. If you're slightly more ambitious you can set up a 'pay as you go' account with other hosting companies and you'll be charged by how much you upload each month and get the RSS feed for free. If you're considerably more ambitious you're looking for your own web server and will probably need an IT professional to help you set it up.

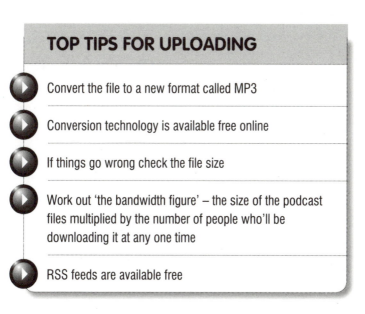

TOP TIPS FOR UPLOADING

- Convert the file to a new format called MP3
- Conversion technology is available free online
- If things go wrong check the file size
- Work out 'the bandwidth figure' – the size of the podcast files multiplied by the number of people who'll be downloading it at any one time
- RSS feeds are available free

QUESTION

- How much space will you need for you pod casts?

ACTION

Multiply the length in minutes by the size of the file you have created and then by the number of episodes to find out how much storage you need.

CHAPTER 8
COPYRIGHT

YouTube with the Performing Rights Society (PRS)

This case study is about the music industry, but it tells a story of a copyright debate that concerns video as well audio rights holders. It focuses on the massive argument about how much should be paid in copyright fees or royalties for music, which resulted in YouTube removing music videos from its site for six months.

The row over how much should be paid when material is copied online began over 50 years ago in those far off days when the music industry started complaining that home taping was killing music. Instead of buying new records, customers were copying the music on their reel-to-reel tape recorders. Then the technology went mobile with the 'Walkman', a small and portable reel-to-reel tape player, and the music industry fought back and made money by creating tapes that customers could buy for their mobile players. But the problem didn't go away. Although in the 1990s the music industry was making massive profits with a new technology, the CD, the industry could not predict how the digital technology that was bringing clearer quality on a compact disc would cause them future problems. Once the material is in a digital format and placed on line, it can be copied without any drop in quality. The record companies were making huge profits by selling CD's but with the growth of the internet, digital online music file sharing became a new threat to their copyright.

Why buy new music when some nice guy has already bought it and will share it with you online? The music file-sharing service Napster had the vision of giving people the opportunity to share MP3 files. The record companies were cut out; the musicians did not receive their royalties. CD sales plummeted. By the early 2000s Napster had been shut down by a US court order, but the floodgates were open and other peer-to-peer file-sharing programmes popped up all over the world wide web. Apple's iPod was the digital 'Walkman' but with storage for thousands of digital tracks. MySpace allowed bands to post music that could be listened to instantly. Spotify created an advertising funded online streaming service, where thousands of tracks and albums can be heard online at no cost.

The organization that represents the record companies in the UK, the BPI (British Phonographic Industry Ltd), estimates that file sharing in Britain alone has cost the industry £200 million a year. What's more this is a worldwide phenomenon. In 2004 global revenue from CD and DVD sales was around $32 billion; by 2012 it's expected to drop to about $11 billion. The sales value of recorded music is falling but the musicians, their managers and producers still need to be paid. So is there a solution?

This is why YouTube stopped showing thousands of official music videos. They argued that the record companies, through the PRS (Performing Rights Society) were asking for outrageously large royalties for placing their music on YouTube. In response the PRS was furious that UK music fans couldn't see the music they love on YouTube for six months while a deal was negotiated. Eventually a deal was struck and licensing agreements with music-streaming websites, such as Spotify and We7, have also been agreed. It's in everyone's interest that the music should be available because research suggests that

> people who file share also buy the most music. The search has begun for new ways of licensing new music technologies rather than continued conflict between the distributors and the rights owners.

Copyright is complicated. Rights in audio and video material are often described in legal documents as being 'in perpetuity throughout all territories in the universe'; it's serious stuff. The key lesson about copyright in this chapter is that it's better to be safe than sorry. If you're in any doubt about who owns rights to what, you need to contact a lawyer; this chapter does not contain legal advice, just guidelines to alert you to common errors.

In the creation of your podcast, whether audio or video, if you've created all the material yourself then you don't have to worry about permissions and copyright. There's no copyright in facts and ideas but there is in the expression and structure of them. If you've included material from other people and haven't got permission to use it, you could get into difficulties. Problems arise not just from using someone else's material but also for allowing others to download it as part of your podcast, as it could be distributed worldwide and 'throughout all the territories in the universe'.

DON'T USE OTHER PEOPLES' WORK WITHOUT THEIR PERMISSION

This chapter focuses on the issues of copyright and trademarks and gives some guidelines on fair trading. Remember www stands for world wide web and that means that anything you post online will be seen worldwide. Internationally, most countries agree with the same key idea that you can't use other people's material without their permission and usually this means you need to pay them for that permission. You should be aware that this may not reflect the exact situation in every territory.

Owning the copyright

You may not be a musician or a TV producer, but as you put your work into digital format and begin to podcast, there's an important question to consider. Do you own the right to show this material to other people? If your aim is to develop your brand through marketing, then the fact that millions of people can view your podcast is a bonus. But if you've created a podcast that uses someone else's material and you've encouraged viewing of material that doesn't belong to you, then you're in trouble. How will the owner make a living from original digital content if you're giving it away for free?

What is copyright?

So, what is copyright? It's a method of protecting creative expression such as written work, music, film, video and pictures. The intellectual property or IP belongs to the expression and to the way it's expressed and is owned by the person who created it. Any work that can be recorded and uploaded online can be protected by copyright. It's worth pointing out here how this is different from a trademark, which is used for a word or an image that distinguish the services of one trader from another. Your podcast can be protected by copyright but if you want to protect the title or name of your podcast, it would need to be registered by a trademark.

Trademarks

If the name or title of your podcast is of particular importance it might be worth checking out the price of registering it as a trademark. Each trademark has to be unique and will be investigated to make sure it's not in conflict with another. In consequence, the cost of registration is high. World Intellectual Property Organization organizes international registrations of trademarks but applications are processed through the applicant's country of origin.

Copyright registration

Copyright registration is easier. The person who created the written work, music, film, video and pictures usually holds the copyright as soon as the work has been recorded and registered. Again, it's worth looking on a country by country basis, and an international registration is available through the Intellectual Property Rights Office's Copyright Registration Service.

QUICK GUIDE TO COPYRIGHT

Start with a copyright notice

'Copyright [dates] by [author/owner]' Some countries use the words 'All Rights Reserved' and you can also use the symbol ©, c of the word copyright in a circle. This copyright notice will advise people that your work is protected.

Common errors

Don't assume that just because some material doesn't appear to have a copyright notice you can use it. If you find something that looks as though no one owns it, that doesn't allow you to use it in your podcast.

Don't assume that because your podcast is free to users that you don't have to pay for copyright. If you're damaging the commercial value of someone else's intellectual property, they will sue you.

Don't assume as well that because the material has been posted online it's therefore available for you to copy. Yes the material is in the 'public domain', but it doesn't belong to you.

The 'Fair Dealing' argument

The argument of 'Fair Dealing or Fair Use' allows users to report news, review books and discuss or comment on work or pictures. It's important because it allows free speech and comment, but that doesn't mean you can copy or use other peoples' material in full; a short accredited excerpt is 'fair'. Legal attitudes to Fair Use are not the same in each territory. Always check.

Common error
It's not considered 'fair use' if you're damaging the original.

Misleading

Think carefully before you name your podcast – you mustn't mislead your podcast users by naming your podcast with a copyright and trademarks that would make them think the material came from a different source, for example, if you're podcasting animation you would be in breach of trademark if you call your business Disney.

Common error
Choosing a name that's already trademarked.

Derivative works

This is material based on or derived from an intellectual property that is exclusive to the original work. This is more likely to occur in written material or audio podcast material, where you've created a story based on an original copyright, eg a sequel using the original characters. If you do it, the owners may sue you for infringement of copyright. Of course they may not, because they might decide you're doing their marketing for them, but it would be safer to check first.

Common error
Thinking it doesn't matter if you borrow someone's work.

Audio copyright – voice

There are two copyright elements to consider if your audio has voice over. First, the copyright in the underlying rights, the actual script or text recorded, and the copyright in the reading or performance or voice. If you're recording an interview with someone, ask for their written permission to podcast the material, making sure they understand how it's going to be podcast.

Common error
Not checking permission for both text and voice.

Audio copyright – music

Performance Rights organizations handle copyright licences for the podcast of musical works, where podcasting counts as a performance. Separate licences are necessary from the originator of the music and from the performers.

Because podcasting is the transmission of a sound recording which is fixed and is accessible on demand by the user it is considered a 'performance'. The copying of the work requires a licence, both for the sound recording and for the musical work. As a podcaster, you can either get a licence from a record company or a performance rights organization or find music that is copyright free. As the popularity of podcasting increases, however, it is fair to assume the performance rights organizations and the record companies will want to make sure their artists receive payment. As explained in the case study, at present they have only tried to control file swapping activities, and in the main focused on the host companies such as Napster. It's likely that in future the law will be clarified on the use of music on podcasts.

Common error
Not taking advantage of music that is specifically licensed for sharing.

Libel and defamation

Podcasters share similar legal risks to broadcasters and newspapers. You can be sued if you say something that is not true; the legal term is defamation, the intentional communication of a false statement about someone to a third party. There are two types of defamation: slander and libel.

1 Slander is an untrue assertion about someone that's spoken.

2 Libel includes untruthful statements expressed in a fixed or permanent medium, such as a podcast, where the statement has the potential to reach a large number of people.

So, always check your facts.

TOP TIP FOR COPYRIGHT

▶ When in doubt, contact a lawyer.

CONNECTING YOUR SKILLS

Not many years ago, if you wanted to make a film you needed a team of at least 10 people. Two to hold the camera, with perhaps an assistant camera person, two to organize the lighting, one to set up the microphones, and one to check the sound levels. You'd also have had a producer, a director, and production manager to write down notes of all the activity and check for mistakes in continuity. Then back at the edit suite there'd be two people waiting to edit the film. Now everything can be done by one person. You. What's more you don't need complicated and heavy equipment, you might have all you need installed on your mobile phone. So you can start straight away.

Of course you're going to feel nervous. You'll have high standards, set by many years of TV viewing where the quality of production is high. But don't worry. The most important element of the podcast is you. Your ideas, and your intellect are what will shine through the material you post online. Web users are not going to turn up their noses because the lighting isn't perfect, or your editing is a little jumpy. In fact they're going to prefer the 'homemade' element of your podcast. Web users will see that it's authentic. In the world of online communications slick professional work isn't valued above genuine expressions of ideas. So get started.

QUESTION

Who does the material for your podcast belong to?

ACTION

You cannot use other people's material without their permission. Podcasters share similar legal risks as broadcasters and newspapers. You can be sued if you say something that is not true.

APPENDIX

DOMAIN NAME, URLS AND HOSTING

If you already have a website you can skip this part of the appendix. But if you were just planning to podcast using a pod delivery service such as iTunes you might not have a site of your own. This appendix gives some quick ideas about what to think about if you're planning your own website.

One of the first things to consider when planning a website where you'll place your podcast is your domain name, which will be part of your web address or, to give it the technical term, URL (Universal Resource Locator).

There are two possible approaches to choosing a name. You could be simply descriptive, but many of the good names have already been taken, especially if you're in a business where there are likely to be many similar traders or practitioners. So you may have to persevere and come up with something more unusual but still, ideally, descriptive of you and your business. The more adjectives you add to the name the more likely you are to succeed in finding a name that hasn't yet been taken. Bear in mind though, that as many customers as you might poach from the other, similarly named site, you could lose even more of your own when they type in your address.

Alternatively, you could take a creative approach and pick a name that's memorable, though it doesn't necessarily have a relevant meaning or anything at all to do with your product. Apple.com is a great example of this, and has sparked many imitators. In theory, the more obscure the name, the less likely it is to be taken, though be warned that many have trodden this path before you and however clever you think you are in picking an obscure, erudite name, someone else will already have snapped up many of the most evocative.

For small companies starting out, who do not yet have a brand name, the most sensible approach is to go for the first kind of domain name, something that's helpfully descriptive of your product or service. It makes your website much easier to find, and more memorable. Don't assume that you need to make your domain name the same as your company's name. If you pick a good domain name that contains a description of your product visitors will still be able to find their way back to the Mark Smith and Sons website. The place to find out what names are available, and to buy the one you want, is through one of the many domain name hosting companies. If you visit one of their websites you'll find the tools to check whether the name you want is available. If it is, you can then buy the right to use that name for a year or more, at a cost of only a few pounds. At the end of the year you'll be asked if you want to renew the domain name. As the cost is rarely more than eight or ten pounds a year, it's often worth hanging on to a good domain name even if your business using that name has temporarily gone on the back burner.

Dot.co.uk or dot.com?

Both these suffixes, the bit that goes at the end of your URL or web address, indicate that the site is going to be primarily in English, though in theory you could build the site in any language you like. So if you choose one of these, the majority of the people who find your site will be English-speaking.

Dot.com used to be the preferred suffix for businesses, because it was among the first to exist and thus suggested you had been trading on the web from the earliest days. Now there are plenty of suffixes to choose from. Some carry more specialist meanings: dot.org suggests non-profit-making organizations and charities, dot.tv, TV companies, dot.edu, schools, dot.ac.uk, British universities. Less specifically you might also consider dot.info and dot.net.

Most people, when choosing their domain name, will at the same time buy up a number of obviously similar ones, including most of the obvious suffixes. The expense is minimal and it is well worth doing to save confusion between your product and someone else's site. Indeed you can buy up as many names as you want and have them all direct people to the same webpage, but clearly you could waste a lot of money if you try to cover every possible permutation. It might be wiser to wait till you are a multi-million-pound global enterprise before you start buying up too many names. For the moment, focus on getting the main website name and URL up and working well.

Choosing the right host company

Domain name hosting companies do more than sell you a name. They also provide you with web space, and thus 'host' your site. So make sure you pick a reliable and reputable company when you start the process of setting up your web address.

There are plenty of tiny web hosts that come and go, but you want a bigger company with staying power and enough customers to be sure they are reputable. Choose a company that's been in business for several years at least. If possible, look for recommendations from anyone you know who has a website.

Most of your communications with them will be via e-mail and the web, but once you are a paying customer there may be telephone support too. The more you pay, the better technical support you'll get. If you're using their least expensive version to set up a website from templates, don't expect much hand-holding.

If you decide to change to a different domain name hosting company, you should still be able to take your domain name with you. It is much the same as switching your phone provider but keeping your number; there will usually be a small additional charge. When you choose a hosting company you need to check that they have the server capacity to host your podcasts.